Back to Me
BTM

The Global Art of Talking Without Listening

By Quentin Drummond Anderson

For the Late Minks Semega Janneh, friend, linguist and great conversationalist.

Copyright Statement

Back to Me: The Global Art of Talking Without Listening

© Quentin Drummond Anderson, 2025

All rights reserved. No part of this publication may be reproduced, stored in a retrieval system, or transmitted in any form or by any means, electronic, mechanical, photocopying, recording, or otherwise, without the prior written permission of the publisher, except in the case of brief quotations embodied in critical articles or reviews.

Publisher's Information

Published by The Writers Collective

First Edition

Cataloguing-in-Publication Data

Anderson, Quentin Drummond Back to Me: The Global Art of Talking Without Listening / Quentin Drummond Anderson

1. Communication—Social aspects
2. Conversation—Cross-cultural studies
3. Listening—Psychology
4. Language and languages—Social aspects
5. Interpersonal communication

Disclaimer

This book is based on observations of contemporary communication practices across multiple cultures. While the author has endeavoured to present accurate cultural perspectives, communication styles are diverse within all cultures, and the observations presented are generalisations intended to illuminate patterns rather than prescribe universal truths.

The views expressed in this book are those of the author and do not necessarily reflect the views of the publisher.

Permissions

For permissions requests beyond the scope of fair use, please contact: The Writers Collective

Table of Contents

Introduction....7

Glossary of Terms....19

1. Welcome to the Echo Chamber....25

2. Interruptus Maximus....35

3. The Monologue Society....43

4. The "As I Was Saying" Species....49

5. Zoom and the Rise of the Talking Head....55

6. Ego in HD....62

7. The Empathy Mirage....69

8. The Psychology of the Unheard....77

9. Loud Men, Loud Women, and the Myth of Balance....83

10. The Pub Philosopher and the Dinner-Table Diplomat....92

11. The Silence Extinction....100

12. The Aggressive Agreeer....108

13. The Feedback Loop of Doom....116

14. When Did Listening Become a Radical Act?....126

15. The Power Pose and the Verbal Flex....134

16. The Politics of Talk....143

17. The Conspiracy of Cleverness....152

18. The Cult of Confidence....161

19. From Dialogue to Duel....168

20. Reclaiming the Pause....176

21. Back to Us....184

Epilogue: The Lunch That Started It All....193

About the Author....196

Sources and Acknowledgements....198

INTRODUCTION: THE AGE OF NOISE

It begins, as most modern tragedies do, with good intentions and Wi-Fi. But before I tell you about the dinner party—and there will be a dinner party—I need to tell you how I arrived at these observations. Because this isn't a book written by someone sitting safely behind an academic desk. This is a book written by someone who has spent thirty years watching the world change, moving through different languages, cultures, and conversational codes, and learning, painfully, that the way we talk to each other matters more than we've ever acknowledged.

In the late 1980s, I was sent by Marsh McLennan—the global risk management company—to the United States. I was young, British, and entirely unprepared for what I was about to learn about how differently people communicate across the Atlantic. It seemed simple enough: same language, same business world. But language, I discovered, is only the surface of conversation. The real substance lies in what remains unsaid, and that unsaid layer varies dramatically from place to place.

In London, I had learned the art of the implied conversation. We said one thing and meant another. Our language was built on understatement, irony, and layers of meaning that required you to understand not just what was said, but what was deliberately left out. A polite "that's an interesting idea" often meant "I think you're completely wrong, but I won't humiliate you by saying so." An English "do what you think is best" could mean anything from "I agree wholeheartedly" to "if you make this decision, I will remember it forever." This was not dishonesty. It was a particular kind of linguistic civility—a form of respect born from a culture that valued restraint.

Then I went to Texas.

In Texas, people said exactly what they meant, and they said it with a friendliness that initially confused me. "Howdy, y'all! How are y'all doing?" strangers would ask, and I would launch into a genuine description of my week before realising they had already moved on. The Texan communication style was warm, direct, and seemingly boundless in its generosity. But there was something I hadn't anticipated: beneath the folksy friendliness was an expectation that you would keep pace, that you would match their energy, that the conversation was a duet that required constant participation. Silence, in Texas, was not a moment of reflection. It was failure to engage.

Then came Los Angeles.

In LA, I encountered a particular brand of conversation where people performed rather than participated. They talked at you, not to you. There was an art to it—a kind of theatrical self-presentation that made listening seem almost irrelevant to the speaker's objectives. People would ask you questions and not wait for answers. They would nod whilst their eyes searched the room for someone more important. The conversation wasn't about connection; it was about positioning. Everyone was always auditioning for something.

And then, unexpectedly, I found myself in New York.

New York hit me with yet another conversational paradigm: aggressive directness wrapped in intellectual combat. In New York, people didn't do warmth or folksy charm. They did sharp, quick-witted exchange. Disagreement wasn't something to avoid with irony or Texas-style friendship. It was foreground.

It was the whole point. New Yorkers interrupted not out of rudeness but out of intellectual engagement. To finish your thought uninterrupted meant they hadn't found it worth interrupting. The conversation was a gladiatorial arena, and if you couldn't defend your position aggressively, you had no right to have expressed it in the first place.

These weren't just regional variations on an American theme. These were completely different languages of interaction, each with its own logic, its own rewards, and its own casualties. But I was only just beginning to understand how varied human conversation could be.

In the 1990s, my career pivoted. I moved into advertising, first with EURO RSCG and later with WPP, and suddenly I was travelling constantly—to Russia, to Asia, to Africa, to every corner of the world where brands were trying to figure out how to sell things to people who didn't speak the same language or share the same cultural references. I thought my American education had prepared me. I was monumentally wrong.

Russia showed me conversation as a chess game—formal, strategic, everything negotiated, nothing assumed. Asia taught me the power of what isn't said at all, where silence carries more weight than words and directness can be read as aggression. Africa revealed the music in conversation, the oral tradition, the way stories and relationships are woven together in ways that the Western world barely recognises as communication at all. With every new geography, every new market, I learned that I knew almost nothing about how people actually talk to each other. What I thought was universal human conversation was actually a series of deeply local conventions, each one perfectly logical from the inside, and utterly foreign from the outside.

By the time I started my own consulting company, I thought I had seen it all. I had travelled enough, worked in enough cultures, absorbed enough different communication styles to understand that conversation is fundamentally context-dependent and culturally determined.

And I realised that everything I had learned about how humans talk to each other was about to become almost irrelevant, because we had built a new layer on top of human conversation, and it had its own language entirely. The language of engineers and data scientists and entrepreneurs and venture capitalists. The language of disruption, of innovation at any cost, of growth metrics and user engagement and algorithmic optimisation. And beneath all of that: the language of velocity. Everything had to be faster. More conversations, shorter conversations, conversations that could be scaled across millions of people simultaneously. There was no time for the African oral tradition. There was no space for the Russian chess-game negotiation. There was no patience for Asian silence. The world had converged on a single conversational style: the one that moved fastest, was loudest, was most easily quantified.

And yet, paradoxically, I was watching something else happen simultaneously. Despite having access to more communication tools than any previous generation in human history—email, texting, video calls, social media, messaging apps—people were reporting being more isolated, more misunderstood, more desperate to be truly heard than ever before.

This is where our dinner party begins.

Picture this scene: you are at a dinner party. Eight reasonably civilised people sit around a carefully decorated table, three bottles of wine stand at various stages of consumption, and the conversation crackles with the kind of energy that only comes when people believe their opinions matter—which, of course, they do, at least to themselves. Someone, perhaps innocently, mentions climate change. Within seconds, the room divides into factions. There is the Eco Warrior, armed with statistics about carbon footprints and renewable energy; the Rational

Economist, prepared to dismantle every point with references to market dynamics; and the Man Who Once Visited Iceland and Now Considers Himself an Expert on Melting Ice Caps, ready to contribute anecdotes about glaciers as if personal observation constitutes peer review. You wait, fork suspended mid-air between plate and mouth, for a pause. Just a small one. A moment in which you might offer a comment—perhaps something nuanced, thoughtfully constructed, and quietly wise. But the pause never comes. No one pauses anymore. Pauses have become extinct, hunted to extinction by the relentless march of our noisy civilisation.

You know the feeling. That moment when you sense the conversational floor opening beneath you, when someone inhales sharply beside you, leans forward with the intensity of a predator, and says: "Actually..." And just like that, your point —whatever it was, however carefully constructed—disappears into the void. The conversation—your conversation, the one you were in the process of having—is hijacked, rebranded, and relaunched under new management. Welcome to the Age of the Conversation Dominator. It is an era defined not by the quality of what we think, but by how loudly we say it. The modern conversationalist is no longer a participant in a mutual exchange; he or she is a performer, forever trapped in the agonising space between self-promotion and self-defence. Every word, every gesture, every laugh is calibrated for effect. Every exchange is a subtle skirmish—a joust of anecdotes, statistics, and carefully curated virtue claims.

If you have ever found yourself nodding politely through someone's monologue whilst your inner voice screams in desperation, "I didn't ask for your TED Talk on the global coffee supply chain," this book is written for you. If you have ever watched someone turn your personal tragedy into their comedic anecdote, you know the feeling. If you have sat through meeting after meeting wondering why no one is actually listening, you are not alone. The phenomenon is not confined to social gatherings or family dinners. It has metastasised across every corner of human interaction. The office Zoom call has become a gladiatorial arena where words are weapons and unmuting is a declaration of war. The family group chat has devolved into a rolling, never-ending debate over who sent the funniest meme, each contribution a bid for attention in a crowded digital space. Even the supposedly tranquil spaces—yoga classes, book clubs, therapy sessions—have been colonised by the verbose and the vehement, those who cannot resist the urge to fill every silence with their own voice.

We are living, simultaneously, in a golden age of articulation and a dark age of attention. Never before in human history have so many people had access to so many platforms on which to express their thoughts. Never before have we been more connected, more capable of reaching vast audiences, more empowered to broadcast our inner lives to the world. And yet, never have we felt more alone, more misunderstood, more desperately craving to be truly heard. This paradox sits at the heart of modern life: we are drowning in voices, yet starving for real communication. Some people blame social media for this catastrophe. They point to that boundless digital echo chamber where the loudest voice inevitably wins and every opinion is, in essence, an audition for relevance. Others point fingers at politics, at the rise of polarisation, at education systems that failed to teach listening. Still others invoke the dopamine economy, the algorithmic manipulation of attention, the structural incentives built into every platform that reward outrage and punish nuance.

But the truth, I believe, is simpler and more unsettling than any of these explanations. We talk to dominate because we are, at our core, terrified of being unheard. In the absence of genuine connection—real, messy, mutual understanding—we fill the silence with ourselves. We talk faster and louder, hoping that volume might somehow compensate for the emptiness beneath. We mistake visibility for value. We confuse volume with virtue. We have somehow managed to build an entire civilisation, from Silicon Valley to Wall Street, from Westminster to Tokyo, on the core conviction that to speak is to exist, and to be silent is to disappear. This is the great lie of our age. And we all believe it.

The rise of what I call the Conversational Narcissist has been swift and, by now, nearly complete. This is the archetypal figure of our time: the person who takes your idea, your hard-won experience, your grief or joy or tragedy, and instantly repackages it as nothing more than a springboard for their own story. You mention, casually, that you have just returned from Italy. Within seconds, they have told you they lived there for a year, know the mayor personally, and have single-handedly reformed the entire Italian olive oil industry. You share that you have had a rough week, that work has been difficult, that you are feeling overwhelmed. They immediately respond by enumerating three worse experiences they have survived, each one more dramatic than the last—involving betrayal, sciatica, and a cat with crippling anxiety. To them, your story is merely the warm-up act for their headline performance. These people do not engage in conversation; they colonise it. They occupy space, consume oxygen, and leave devastation in their wake. Yet curiously— and this is the great tragedy—they thrive everywhere. In the boardroom and the pub, at the dinner table and the family reunion, they are rewarded, elevated, and often genuinely admired. Why? Because society has come to reward noise over nuance. Because confidence, even when catastrophically misplaced, trumps reflection every single time. Because the loud are perceived as leaders while the quiet are dismissed as uncertain.

So why do people dominate conversations? The reasons are rarely as simple as arrogance or malice. Many chronic dominators are, paradoxically, deeply insecure. Their relentless verbosity is not confidence; it is armour. It is a carefully constructed defence mechanism, a way of avoiding the terrifying possibility of exposure. Silence frightens them more than almost anything else, because silence invites thought, and thought invites doubt. Their own doubt. So the constant, relentless stream of words becomes a buffer against the terror of irrelevance. In an attention economy—which is to say, in the economy in which we now all live—to stop speaking is, quite literally, to disappear. To be silent is to cease to exist. But there is another reason for the dominance of the dominator, one that is more cultural than psychological: we have thoroughly confused volume with value. From politics to podcasts, from social media influencers to corporate boardrooms, visibility has somehow become the new virtue. You do not need to be right. You do not need to be wise. You do not even need to be particularly intelligent. You just need to be relentless. You need to keep talking, regardless of what you are saying. The world, it seems, will reward you for it.

Once upon a time, in cultures across the world, conversation was considered an art form worthy of study and refinement. There were rhythms to it, courtesies and unspoken rules that governed the flow. In Paris, in Tokyo, in Cairo, in Dublin—and yes, even in London, Texas, and New York—people understood, either intuitively or through explicit training, that dialogue required patience, timing, and the genuine willingness to be transformed by what someone else had to say. There were pauses. There was breathing. There was space for thought. Different cultures had different ways of creating that space, but the space itself was universally respected. Today, conversation more closely resembles a race: who can seize the microphone first? Who can keep it longest? Who can shout over the competition? Listening, that ancient and now seemingly obsolete skill, has become a genuinely radical act—the conversational equivalent of slow food in a world of fast-food drive-throughs. It is viewed with suspicion, as though the person who listens must be weak, slow, insufficiently confident in their own opinions. Yet the irony is exquisite, and it is worth dwelling on: those who truly listen—who give space rather than seize it, who ask questions rather than make declarations—are the ones who command the most genuine respect. Great negotiators, therapists, wise leaders, and the people we actually want to be around all understand this paradox: the most powerful person in the room is often the quietest. They do not dominate through volume; they draw others in through the extraordinary gift of genuine attention.

What we have lost, in our rush to be heard, is the possibility of actually understanding one another. We have confused communication with transmission. We think the goal is simply to get our message out, when the actual goal—the real goal—should always be to create genuine understanding. We measure success by volume rather than by impact. We ask ourselves: "How many people heard me?" rather than "Did anyone truly understand what I was trying to say?" We are living through what might be called the Age of Transmission, where everyone has their own channel, their own platform, their own amplified voice, but nobody—and I mean nobody—is actually having a conversation anymore. The architecture of modern life has been designed, almost deliberately, to prevent real dialogue.

So what can we do about this? The obvious solutions seem either impossible or cruel. Should we ban the talkers? Install conversational timers in every dining room? Introduce a "word quota" per social gathering? Tempting, but perhaps too draconian. Instead, what this book offers is something gentler, something more hopeful: a rebellion. Not a violent revolution, but a quiet one. It is a call to reclaim the pause—that terrifying, beautiful, empty space between one person's words and another's. It is a call to reclaim the question, posed with genuine curiosity rather than rhetorical flourish. It is a call to reclaim the open ear, the willingness to be changed by what you hear. Because here is the truth that the noisy world does not want you to know: when everyone shouts, wisdom whispers. And if wisdom is ever to be heard again in this loud, relentless world, someone must finally, courageously, be willing to listen.

By the end of this journey through the architecture of modern conversation, you will find that Back to Me becomes a kind of mirror—an uncomfortable mirror, yes, but a necessary one. It forces us to ask not just about who dominates, but crucially, when do we? After all, the line between conversational victim and conversational villain is far thinner than we would like to admit. We are all of us, occasionally, the interrupter who cannot wait for someone to finish. We have all been, at some moment, the monologuer who did not notice the glaze in someone's eyes. We have all committed the sin of the "As I Was Saying" offender —that terrible moment when someone tries to return to their original point and we simply do not have the grace to let them. But recognising it—truly catching ourselves mid-monologue, mid-interruption, mid-performance—is the first step towards something better. It is the first step towards genuine civility, towards authentic empathy, and towards a more human kind of communication altogether.

And perhaps, one day soon, we will find ourselves sitting at a table where conversation flows like good wine—freely, generously, without performance or calculation, and most importantly, without anyone shouting Back to Me! This book is an exploration of how we arrived at this noisy, disconnected moment. It is an investigation into what we have lost in the process of gaining all these platforms and microphones and opportunities to be heard. But most importantly, it is an argument for recovery. It is a map towards reclaiming something essential about what it means to be human: the capacity to be changed by another person's story. The willingness to be wrong. The courage to be quiet. The radical act of actually listening to someone else. This is not a self-help book, though you may find help in it. This is not a treatise on communication theory, though theory will emerge from the conversations we examine. This is an invitation to look at the world as it actually is—loud, distracted, urgent, desperate to be heard—and to ask yourself: is this really how we want to communicate? And if not, what will it take to change?

QUENTIN DRUMMOND ANDERSON

THE GLOSSARY

The Actually Person

A walking correction engine who lies dormant until you say something vaguely interpretable. Then—pounce—"Actually…"
Goal: Prove omniscience.
Result: You forget what you were trying to say.

Interruptus Maximus

A majestic species that interrupts before your thought has fully hatched.
Key Behaviour: Treats your sentence like a race they must win by starting before you finish.
Warning: They can smell a pause from several feet away.

The Monologue Society

A vast, informal network of people who believe conversations are just speeches with worse lighting.
Atmosphere: TED Talk meets hostage situation.
Listener Response: Dissociation by minute eight.

The "As I Was Saying" Species

These tenacious beings cannot accept that a story might naturally die. Their life mission is to return the entire group to a half-finished anecdote from 40 minutes ago.
Signature Move: "Anyway… as I was saying…"

The Aggressive Agreeer

Overwhelms you not with contradiction, but with violently enthusiastic agreement that instantly shifts the spotlight onto them.
Impact: You share a story; they share a saga.

The One-Upper

Capable of turning even your most mundane achievement into a springboard for their far superior version.
Example:
You: "I'm tired."
Them: "Oh, I haven't slept since 2014."

The Data Dropper

A statistical sniper. They lurk quietly until unleashing a devastating barrage of studies, charts, or research papers that invalidate your lived experience.
Favourite Phrase: "Well, actually, research shows…"

The Conversational Narcissism Index (CNI)

A unit of measurement indicating how many seconds it takes a person to turn any topic back to themselves.
Scoring Guide:

* 10 seconds: Troubling
* 5 seconds: Problematic
* 2 seconds: Advanced
* 0 seconds: Should not be invited to anything

The Cognitive Magpie

Distracted by mental "shiny objects," this thinker cannot stay on a topic for more than three seconds before veering into a totally unrelated anecdote.
Effect: Conversational teleportation.

The Empathy Mirage

Appears deeply understanding—tilted head, soft eyes, perfect nodding—but retains none of the actual content of your speech.
Discovery: They ask the same question you just answered 3 minutes earlier.

Authenticity Theatre

A fully choreographed performance of vulnerability designed to appear spontaneous.
Warning Signs:

"I'm just going to be really real for a second…"
 A perfectly timed tear.

The Polite Ambusher

Interrupts with such shocking manners that you don't realise you've been silenced until several hours later.
Opening Line: "Sorry, may I just add—"
And suddenly you no longer exist.

Silence Extinction

The modern condition in which pauses—once meaningful—are now viewed as emergencies requiring immediate verbal filling.
Cause:Societal fear of thought.
Side Effects: Endless babble.

The Feedback Loop of Doom

Occurs when two or more people enthusiastically agree themselves into an escalating spiral of overconfidence.
Stages:

"Yes!" → "Exactly!" → "Absolutely!" → "We're geniuses!"
Destination:** Catastrophic certainty.

Why This Glossary Matters More Than Ever

Because without it, how would we describe the daily conversational chaos that leaves us confused, exhausted, and contemplating early retirement from human interaction?

This glossary isn't just helpful—it's humanitarian.
It arms you with language, awareness, and the ability to point at a situation and mutter, "Ah yes… classic Interruptus Maximus.We have been waiting for you."

And honestly? That alone makes life easier.

QUENTIN DRUMMOND ANDERSON

CHAPTER ONE: WELCOME TO THE ECHO CHAMBER

The hijacking and rebranding of conversation

It starts with a voice—but not yours. You are halfway through making a point. It is something intelligent, perhaps even a little profound. You have thought about it. You have rehearsed it in your mind. The words are chosen carefully, the argument structured logically, and you are just reaching the moment where you will deliver the insight that ties everything together. Then, suddenly, you feel it. That faint, almost imperceptible social shiver that passes through the air like a current of electricity. Someone beside you inhales sharply. They lean forward. Their entire body language shifts from listening to launching. And they say, with the force of absolute certainty: "Actually..." And just like that, the floor disappears beneath your argument. The conversation—your conversation, the one you were in the process of having, the one to which you have contributed your time and thought—is hijacked. It is rebranded. It is relaunched under entirely new management. The "Actually Person" has arrived. They do not ask permission. They do not wait for you to finish. They simply seize the moment and make it theirs.

We have all met them. Some of us, if we are honest with ourselves, have been them—at least once, at least occasionally, at least when we were tired or nervous or desperate to prove something. They dominate panels, hijack family dinners, and hold forth in pubs as though they are auditioning for a radio slot that no one has actually offered them. They are the emperors of interruption, the monarchs of monologue, the undisputed kings and queens of the conversational realm. They take up space. They consume oxygen. They leave other people feeling somehow diminished, as though their own thoughts and experiences have been deemed insufficient, unsophisticated, unworthy of the group's collective attention. And they are everywhere. In the office, in the café, in the classroom, in the family WhatsApp group, in the comments section of every social media post. They have achieved a kind of ubiquity that is nothing short of remarkable. One might even wonder whether we have reached a tipping point in human civilisation where the ability to dominate a conversation has become not just an individual trait but a cultural value, actively cultivated and rewarded.

We are living through the loudest period in human history—and I do not mean loudest in terms of decibels, though certainly the world is noisier than it has ever been. I mean loudest in terms of declarations. Every platform, every device, every dinner table has become an open microphone. Everyone has an opinion. Everyone believes, with absolute conviction, that they are entitled to express it. And everyone—without exception—seems to believe that silence is an unnatural state, something to be avoided at all costs, a failure rather than a choice. The technology that surrounds us conspires to keep us talking. Algorithms nudge us towards sharing. Notifications buzz constantly, demanding our attention and response. Podcasts babble endlessly in the background of our lives. We have created an entire civilisation, with its structures and incentives and cultural values, built on a single assumption: the worst thing one can be is unheard. The worst fate is invisibility. The ultimate sin is silence.

We tweet. We post. We pontificate. We mistake the hum of self-expression for genuine connection. Yet the irony—and it is an irony so profound that it borders on tragic—is exquisite: the more we speak, the less we listen. The more platforms we have for our voices, the fewer people are actually paying attention to what anyone is saying. We have optimised for transmission at the expense of reception. We have designed systems that make it easier to broadcast than to understand. The result is a kind of collective alienation, a world in which we are all shouting into the void, convinced that our message matters while simultaneously suspecting that no one is actually hearing us. The louder we get, the more isolated we feel. The more we talk, the lonelier we become.

The modern talker is a curious species—part performer, part preacher, part minor philosopher. They possess an unshakeable belief that they have something important to say, regardless of whether they actually do. Their confidence is magnetic, almost hypnotic. Their certainty is unbreakable. And their need for validation is as bottomless as a politician's promises. But perhaps their defining characteristic—the thing that truly sets them apart—is their subtle, almost invisible disdain for the concept of turn-taking. For them, conversation is not an exchange between equals. It is not a mutual exploration of ideas. It is a stage. A platform. An opportunity for performance. Other people's words are merely the warm-up acts to their headline performance. They are useful insofar as they provide a springboard for the talker's next monologue, but they are not intrinsically valuable. They are not worth listening to. You can see this in the talker's eyes. There is an impatient flicker there while you are speaking—a kind of restless energy barely contained. There is a slight tilt of the head that seems to say: I am not listening. I am loading. I am preparing my next interruption. I am thinking about how I can turn this back to me.

How did we get here? Once upon a time, in every culture across the world, conversation was understood as a civilised dance. There were rhythms to it. There were courtesies and unspoken rules that governed the flow. People understood, perhaps through explicit teaching or perhaps through observation and cultural osmosis, that conversation required patience. It required timing. It required genuine interest in what the other person had to say. People took turns. They exchanged ideas. They listened. Crucially, they listened. Now, conversation resembles something closer to a mosh pit—chaotic, aggressive, potentially dangerous, with everyone fighting for space and air. The shift began, innocently enough, with the democratisation of self-expression. We were told, from childhood onwards, that it was healthy to "find our voice." Schools encouraged it. Corporations hired consultants to teach it. Self-help books promised that personal transformation was impossible without it. So we did. We found our voices. We leaned in. We owned the rooms. We spoke up at meetings. We started blogs and podcasts and social media accounts. We spoke. And then we kept speaking.

What began as empowerment—a genuine movement to give voice to the voiceless—became something else entirely. The right to speak, which is genuinely important and worth fighting for, mutated into a right to dominate. The commitment to listening to all voices somehow became permission to hear only one's own. And before long, the loudest person at the table was not just heard—they were rewarded. They were promoted. They were celebrated. They were held up as an example of what success looks like. We began to equate volume with value. Confidence became synonymous with competence. The quiet, reflective type—the person who thinks before speaking, who listens carefully, who considers multiple perspectives—became "low-energy." They were dismissed as "passive." They were regarded with suspicion. Meanwhile, the loud, opinionated, aggressive talker was seen as "confident." "Charismatic." "Leadership material." Society confused confidence with competence, and we have been drowning in hot air ever since. The consequences have been catastrophic.

In a world where everyone is talking, silence feels like surrender.

It feels like failure. It feels like weakness. So we adapt. We learn to fight back. We learn to defend our conversational territory. The person who was once content to be a gentle conversationalist—to listen more than speak, to ask questions, to allow others their moment—must now become a strategist. You must calculate. You must plan. Pause too long, and someone will seize your slot, your moment, your opportunity to be heard. Show any hint of uncertainty, and a nearby expert will pounce, correcting you, reframing your point, turning it into their own. Express empathy or vulnerability, and the monologuer will mistake it for an invitation to continue, an opening to delve deeper into their own story, their own experience, their own pain or triumph. Thus, the conversational arms race begins. To survive, we interrupt preemptively. We fill gaps compulsively. We raise our voices imperceptibly louder each time we speak, trying to cut through the noise, trying to be heard, trying to matter.

The result is a strange kind of chaos—everyone broadcasting simultaneously, no one receiving. It is like trying to hold a conversation in a room where every single person is wearing a megaphone. The noise builds and builds. It becomes overwhelming. And yet people keep shouting, convinced that if they just speak louder, faster, more cleverly, their message will finally break through. It does not. What is most tragic—and most comic—about this entire phenomenon is that the great conversational dominators truly believe they are "connecting." They genuinely think that their endless talking, their relentless interrupting, their constant steering of the conversation back to themselves is a form of engagement. They mistake attention for affection. They confuse domination with dialogue. They think their ability to tell a good story, to deliver a punch line, to hold forth on a topic with apparent expertise somehow makes them interesting. It does not. It makes them exhausting. It makes people want to avoid them. It makes dinner parties feel like endurance tests rather than pleasant social occasions.

There is a fine line between being engaging and being unbearable. The conversation dominator crosses that line with Olympic regularity. You can spot them—often identify them before they even open their mouth—by their catchphrases. "Let me just stop you there..." they will say, before you have barely finished your sentence. "That reminds me of something I did..." they will announce, completely changing the subject to something that relates only tangentially to what was being discussed, and only because it provides a platform for their own story. "You will laugh," they will say—though you almost certainly will not—"this is about me, actually." They frame their interruptions as helpful. They present their monologues as contributions to the conversation. They believe, genuinely, that they are adding value. They mean no harm, of course. They are not deliberately cruel or malicious. They are simply unable to imagine a world not arranged around their own commentary. They are the protagonists of their own perpetual podcast, and everyone else exists in their narrative as supporting characters.

The digital world has weaponised this conversational tendency. It has taken something that was always present in human nature—the desire to be heard, to matter, to have one's experiences validated—and has industrialised it. Where once you had to interrupt someone in person, an act requiring a certain amount of courage, breath control, and social risk, you can now do it asynchronously, at massive scale, and without any real consequence. On social media, conversation is not dialogue. It is parallel monologue. Every opinion exists in splendid isolation, punctuated only by emoji applause or outrage. Instagram, LinkedIn, TikTok—all of these platforms reward performance over genuine participation. Even the platforms that were explicitly built on conversation—designed with the intention of creating dialogue—quickly devolve into ego-fests. You see endless panels of people speaking at one another, each one convinced they are changing the world, when in fact they are simply rearranging their own sentences, their own thoughts, their own carefully curated personas.

We have become so accustomed to the sound of our own voices—so inured to the constant background noise of self-promotion and self-expression—that silence now feels genuinely threatening. It feels like an existential crisis. An empty space in a conversation feels like a failure that must be immediately remedied. An unanswered text feels like abandonment. A pause in a meeting feels like an opportunity being lost. We have wired ourselves to be uncomfortable with quiet. We have created technologies that punish silence and reward constant contribution. We have built a world in which the unspoken is treated as suspicious. Picture the scene. It is a dinner party. Eight guests sit around a table that has been carefully set, thoughtfully decorated, prepared with the host's best intentions. The conversation turns to travel. Someone mentions, lightly and conversationally, that they have just returned from Greece. Within seconds—literally within seconds—the table explodes with counter-stories. One guest "simply must tell you" about their Mykonos villa, as though the fact that they have visited Greece several times somehow makes them an expert on the country. Another delivers an unsolicited, lengthy lecture on Greek debt-to-GDP ratios, as though macroeconomic policy is the appropriate response to a travel anecdote. A third interrupts both of them to explain why Crete is "underrated, if you know the right people"—the implication being that they do know the right people, and therefore their experience is somehow more authentic, more valuable, more worth hearing than anyone else's.

You try to smile. You take a sip of your wine. You briefly, almost unconsciously, entertain the fantasy of throwing your dessert spoon into the nearest glass of water, creating a small but significant disturbance that might restore order to the conversation. But it will not work. Because conversation, in the modern sense, is no longer about mutual exchange. It is about possession. Who owns the moment? Whose voice fills the space? Whose narrative becomes the frame through which everyone else's experience is understood? You leave the dinner slightly dazed. You cannot remember a single fact that anyone shared. You cannot recall any new information you learned or any interesting perspective you had not considered. But you are acutely, painfully aware that everyone at that table left the dinner believing they had been fascinating. They had successfully dominated. They had won.

The cult of "authenticity" has not helped matters. We are now told, constantly and from every direction, that to speak one's mind—loudly, often, and without restraint—is the highest moral virtue. To filter your thoughts is to betray yourself. To consider how your words might land is to be inauthentic. To think before speaking is to be dishonest. This is a corrosive philosophy. But unfiltered expression is not authenticity. It is indulgence. It is selfishness dressed up in the language of honesty. Authenticity without empathy is just noise with better branding. It is ego with a social justice coating. The true art of communication has never been in declaring who we are. It has always been in discovering who someone else is. But that requires listening. It requires genuine curiosity. It requires the willingness to be changed by what you hear. These are skills that our noisy civilisation has systematically failed to teach.

Every now and then, however, you meet a genuine listener. They are rare. Almost mythical. Like unicorns, but better dressed and more likely to actually exist. They look you in the eye. They wait for you to finish your thought—and I mean genuinely finish, not just pause for breath so they can launch into their own narrative. They do not rush to insert themselves into your story or try to top your anecdote with one of their own. They understand —truly understand—that the real pleasure of conversation is not in talking. It is in witnessing thought unfold. It is in being present for someone else's moment of vulnerability or insight. Around such people, even the chronic dominators falter. Their rhythms collapse. Their usual patterns of interruption and domination suddenly feel awkward, inappropriate. Their noise begins to sound hollow and transparent. Because genuine listening, done well and with true presence, is disarming. It draws power not through display but through stillness. It gains influence not through interruption but through attention. It is not submission. It is strategy. It is the most sophisticated move in any social game.

The final irony is this: the problem is not them. The dominators, the interrupters, the monopolisers of conversational space. The problem is us. Every single time we reward the loud, every time we equate aggression with intelligence, every time we give the microphone to the person who shouts loudest, we reinforce the behaviour. Every "great point" muttered in response to someone's monologue feeds the beast. Every laugh at an interrupted joke encourages more interruption. Every promotion given to the loudest voice in the room sends a message to everyone else: keep talking, ignore others, dominate or be dominated. And, if we are honest with ourselves, we all have a little dominator within us. We all have that itchy impatience when we are waiting for someone to finish speaking so we can reclaim the stage. We all have that reflexive "Back to Me!" impulse that arises when someone else dares to shine. We all occasionally fail to notice the person trying to speak in the corner. We all sometimes mistake our own voice for the sound of the world.

The only cure for this epidemic is awareness. The only antidote is irony. Once you see the pattern—really see it—you cannot unsee it. Once you catch yourself doing it—mid-interruption, mid-monologue, mid-performance—you cannot quite bear it. And that—faintly, quietly, almost imperceptibly—is the beginning of change. Not dramatic change, not revolutionary transformation, but something slower and more sustainable. A shift in awareness. A moment of recognition. A choice to do something different the next time you feel that urge to interrupt. To dominate. To steer the conversation back to yourself.

We live in an age of permanent conversation, yet we are chronically misunderstood. We have built a world that prizes the confident statement over the considered silence. We have created systems and structures that reward certainty and punish doubt. But conversation, at its best, is not combat. It is not a competition. It is choreography. It requires rhythm. It requires humility. It requires the willingness to yield, to be surprised, to be changed. The dominator—poor, exhausting soul—will never know the beauty of that dance. But perhaps, if we listen hard enough, if we resist the constant pressure to speak, if we cultivate the radical discipline of silence, we still can.

CHAPTER TWO: INTERRUPTUS MAXIMUS -HOW TO LOSE FRIENDS AND DOMINATE CONVERSATIONS

Seizing control of the Space

There are many ways to interrupt someone. Some are bold and unmistakable, like a cavalry charge across a conversational battlefield. Others are so artfully disguised that they could pass for politeness. Some interruptions feel like genuine engagement, while others land like a slap. But all of them—regardless of their style or finesse—share a single purpose: to seize control of the conversational space before your opponent realises a war has even begun. In the modern world, interruption is not merely a bad habit or a minor social transgression. It is a global sport. Every culture plays it differently, with its own rules, its own rhythms, and its own weapons. The British interrupt apologetically. The Americans interrupt enthusiastically. The Italians interrupt passionately. The French interrupt philosophically. And the Finns, quietly baffled by all of this, interrupt not at all—instead, they wait, they listen, and when they finally speak, everyone falls silent.

But what unites all these different cultural styles is something revealing about humanity itself: how a culture views power, politeness, and the value of silence says everything about what that culture values. When you understand a society's interruption style, you understand its soul.

Consider the British interruption. No nation interrupts quite like the British—softly, apologetically, and usually with the word "sorry" embedded somewhere in the interruption itself. The British interrupter is a master of stealth, a ninja of social nicety. They will not grab the floor outright; that would be vulgar, crude, and entirely un-British. Instead, they will sneak onto the conversational stage through a side door of civility. "Sorry to cut across you, but—" they will say, with genuine sorrow in their voice, as though they are pained by the necessity of interrupting you. "I completely see your point, but might I just add—" they will suggest, in a tone that implies they are not so much interrupting as gently enhancing. "Fascinating, fascinating," they will murmur with apparent sincerity, "although one could argue—" and just like that, they have landed their counter-argument. By the time you realise you have been interrupted, they have already framed their point, quoted the Financial Times, and poured themselves another cup of tea.

This genteel aggression is deeply cultural. It is the product of centuries of British tradition, of a society that values hierarchy but pretends it does not exist, of a people who have perfected the art of saying devastating things while smiling pleasantly. The British conversation is a delicate dance of understatement and hierarchy—a social game where blunt interruption is frowned upon, yet subtle dominance is not only expected but required. To speak too long is vulgar. To say too little is weak. You must find the narrow path between the two, neither dominating nor submitting, but always, always maintaining your position in the invisible hierarchy. So the British have evolved what might be the most exquisite of all conversational weapons: the polite ambush. The apology that is not an apology. The interruption that sounds like collaboration. The dominance that masquerades as deference.

Across the Atlantic, interruption takes on an entirely different character. In the United States, interruption is not a sin—it is an act of engagement. In America, to interrupt is to care. It shows enthusiasm, energy, and confidence. It demonstrates that you are invested in the conversation. The phrase "I love that!"

is usually followed by a complete change of subject, and yet it is delivered with such warmth that it feels like a compliment rather than a hijacking. American conversations resemble a jazz improvisation: loud, overlapping, full of competing solos. The goal is not harmony—it is presence. Everyone wants to be the saxophone. Everyone is playing at the same time. The conversations are exhilarating, chaotic, and utterly exhausting to anyone raised in a more orderly tradition.

This stems from the American national creed of self-expression. From kindergarten onwards, children are taught to "speak up," to share their thoughts, to value their opinions. Every teacher encourages participation. Every corporate coaching session emphasises the importance of "finding your voice." Every motivational speaker promises that your unique perspective is valuable and needs to be heard. As a result, Americans have turned interruption into something approaching a patriotic art form. They are not trying to dominate—at least not consciously. They are trying to connect. But somewhere between enthusiasm and ego, somewhere in the gap between good intention and actual impact, genuine connection gets lost in the static. What was meant to be engagement becomes noise.

In France, by contrast, interruption is executed with surgical precision and intellectual grace. The French interrupt with elegance—a conversational duel conducted with the precision of épée fencing. To interrupt is not rude; it is proof of intellect. It means you are thinking, engaging, actively refining ideas in real time. In Parisian dinner parties, overlap is oxygen. A silent guest is a social corpse. Where the Anglo-Saxon ideal prizes listening as a fundamental virtue, the French consider it a conversational sin to let an idea stagnate unchallenged. Every remark invites a riposte. Every opinion demands a counter-thought. The result is exhilarating and exhausting in equal measure. You leave feeling both enlightened and slightly wounded, as though you have been intellectually sparred with by someone who is genuinely better at thinking than you are. It is competitive, yes, but it is also a form of respect. They would not bother interrupting if they did not think you were worth engaging with.

Italian conversation, by contrast, is not linear—it is symphonic. Everyone talks at once. Voices rise and fall like an orchestral piece. Hands conduct invisible orchestras. Gestures punctuate speech as much as words do. To interrupt in Italy is not to offend; it is to participate. Silence implies disinterest, which is the greatest insult of all. It is a language of rhythm, emotion, and volume, where passion outweighs protocol and enthusiasm trumps formal politeness. The Italian interrupter does not steal your line; they join your aria. They amplify it. They take your thought and make it bigger, louder, more operatic. Foreigners often mistake this for chaos. Italians call it conversation.

Then there are the Nordic countries—those rare pockets of humanity where silence is not awkward but sacred. In Sweden, Norway, and Finland, pauses are not conversational failures; they are breathing spaces for thought. A Finnish person will listen quietly, wait several seconds, and then deliver one perfectly chosen sentence that ends the discussion entirely. To interrupt here is social vandalism. The silence carries its own grammar. To fill it needlessly is to expose insecurity or, worse, to show disrespect. For anyone raised in louder cultures, a Nordic conversation can feel like a philosophical endurance test. You speak. You wait. Then, if you are lucky, someone nods. But beneath that stillness lies an elegant truth: power does not always require noise. Sometimes the person who speaks least wields the most influence.

If you map Europe by conversational temperature, you find the Mediterranean nations glowing red-hot while the north stays pale blue. In Italy, Spain, and Greece, interrupting shows warmth. It is a sign you are engaged. In Denmark or Germany, it signals aggression. It is a matter of rhythm and cultural expectation, not rudeness per se. In the south, talking over someone is a form of intimacy—proof you care enough to fight for your point. In the north, it is social violence. One Italian academic once told me, with a characteristically Italian shrug, "We interrupt because we care. If we do not interrupt, we do not like you." A Swede would find that deeply traumatic. Yet they are both right, from their own cultural perspective. The interruption means something completely different depending on the context in which it occurs.

In much of East and Southeast Asia, the dynamic reverses entirely. Speech is hierarchical. Age, seniority, and social position dictate the conversational tempo and who gets to speak. To interrupt a superior—or even a peer—can be an act of profound disrespect. Harmony matters more than individual expression. Hierarchy matters more than equality. So interruption is rare, but when it happens, it carries weight. Here, silence is not weakness but strength. The listener gains moral authority through restraint. The speaker carries the burden of maintaining harmony. It is why Western executives, when dropped into a Tokyo boardroom, often mistake reflective silence for disinterest. In reality, it is deep engagement, just expressed through the absence of noise rather than the presence of it. Where Western conversation rewards dominance, Eastern conversation values control—the ability to speak when appropriate, to stay silent when necessary, to read the room and adjust accordingly.

In the Middle East, conversation is communal and fluid, deeply performative. In the majlis—the traditional sitting room where important conversations happen—everyone speaks, everyone listens, and everyone interrupts, but with grace. A guest's interruption is not an insult; it is a sign of shared energy. Here, dominance is less about noise and more about narrative. Who can tell the best story? Who can quote the wisest saying? Who can deliver the most generous hospitality while speaking? It is interruption as choreography, not combat. It is the art of interruption refined through centuries of tradition.

In the Balkans, meanwhile, a unique blend of Slavic candour and Mediterranean intensity creates something entirely different. Here, monologues are delivered with the force of personal testimony and the rhythm of dark comedy. People speak as if addressing both you and history itself. Every story is a protest, a poem, and a punchline. The listener nods, smokes, and occasionally interjects with a "You think that's bad?" before launching into their own chapter. It is chaos, but glorious chaos. Conversation as catharsis. Everyone in the room has a story. Everyone believes their story matters. Everyone interrupts to prove their point. And somehow, it works. Somehow, the conversation moves forward. Somehow, community is maintained despite the noise.

What all this reveals is something fundamental: "rudeness" is deeply relative. The very act that wins admiration in one culture provokes horror in another. In Britain, cutting someone off mid-sentence might ruin a friendship. In Brazil, it might mean you are finally getting along. In Poland, it might be proof you are paying attention. We interpret interruption through our own cultural lenses, and when those lenses do not match, misunderstanding is inevitable. The British think Americans are brash. The Americans think the British are repressed and passive-aggressive. The Italians think everyone else is dead inside. And the Finns, quietly, think we are all ridiculous—all this noise, all this fighting for space, when a simple nod and a cup of coffee would suffice.

Globalisation has made this worse. In international meetings, the clash of conversational codes is a silent battlefield. Picture it: a conference call between New York, London, Stockholm, and Milan. The Americans leap in enthusiastically, the British murmur "If I might," the Swedes wait for a pause that never comes while the Italians join midway through, already in full voice, conducting the conversation like a symphony that only they can hear. Everyone thinks everyone else is being rude. Everyone is convinced they are just trying to communicate normally. Everyone is frustrated. The result is not dialogue—it is Babel with broadband.

Why do we interrupt? Across all borders, the impulse shares one root: the desire for recognition. We interrupt not because we are cruel or thoughtless, but because we are desperate to be understood. We are terrified of being ignored. Interruption is anxiety in motion—the fear that our thought will evaporate if not expressed immediately. It is the terror that if we do not speak now, we will lose our opportunity forever. It is also the purest form of ego: the conviction that whatever we are about to say matters more than what is being said now. The tragedy is that most interrupters believe they are helping. They think they are building on your point, adding energy, validating your view. They do not realise they have just kidnapped your sentence and left it for dead on the roadside.

In the digital age, attention is the new currency—and interruption is its inflation. The more we fight to be heard, the less anyone actually hears. Every platform, every meeting, every public debate has become a competition for mental bandwidth. We interrupt not just with words, but with notifications, feeds, alerts, and constant self-promotion. We are, in effect, living inside one vast, global interruption—a never-ending chorus of everyone shouting "Back to me!"

What, then, is the antidote? Perhaps it is cultural humility. Learning from those who still value the pause. The Nordic stillness. The Japanese restraint. The Arabian hospitality. All of these remind us that conversation is not a contest but a collaboration. To pause is not to lose the floor. It is to hold it with quiet authority. It is to say, without words, that what matters more than winning is understanding. That is the real revolution.

The empire of interruption thrives in every climate. Its plumage varies—polite in Britain, exuberant in Brazil, deadly precise in France—but its purpose is universal: to reclaim attention, to assert importance, to say loudly and clearly that I matter. We live, after all, in the Age of the Echo—a world where silence is suspect and speech is survival. And yet, as any wise Finn or thoughtful observer of human nature could tell us, the greatest dominance of all is not in speaking first. It is in being the one everyone wants to speak to. It is in listening so well that people trust you with their deepest thoughts. It is in creating space so safe that others can finally relax and be themselves. That is power. That is real influence. That is what the interrupters, in all their loud glory, have not yet learned.

CHAPTER THREE: THE MONOLOGUE SOCIETY- WHEN TALKING REPLACED THINKING

The trapping of humanity

It used to be that conversation was a dialogue. Now it is a broadcast. Everywhere you look—in offices and cafés, in podcasts and classrooms, in living rooms and lecture halls—humanity seems to be trapped in one vast monologue, a theatre of perpetual self-expression where the curtain never falls and the audience has long since left the building. We have become performers in a world without an audience. We are all soliloquising into the void, convinced that our voice matters, that our perspective is unique, that the world desperately needs to hear what we have to say. In this age of abundance—of microphones, comment sections, streaming platforms, and personal branding opportunities—everyone has a platform, but few have anything truly new to say. It is not that we have lost the art of conversation. It is that we have mistaken talking for communicating. You see it everywhere: the influencer talking to camera as though possessed by a spirit, the corporate manager delivering a "town hall" to rows of employees who would rather be anywhere else, the dinner guest recounting their sabbatical in Bali as if they were Shackleton returning from the Antarctic with a yoga mat. We live not in the Information Age, but the Declaration Age. It is no longer enough to think—one must announce that one is thinking. It is no longer sufficient to have an experience—one must broadcast it, comment on it, monetise it, and wait for the validation of strangers.

The Anglo-American world, naturally, leads the charge into this new territory. From London to Los Angeles, from Silicon Valley to the City of London, speech has become a performance of confidence. At the British dinner table, people perform modesty with the precision of a stage actor: "Oh, I probably shouldn't say this, but—" (translation: I have been waiting all night to say this, and I will say it now with great pleasure). The conversation follows a carefully choreographed dance of understatement and superiority. Across the Atlantic, the American variant replaces irony with enthusiasm. Conversations are motivational seminars. Even apologies come with a PowerPoint presentation. The performance is optimistic, high-energy, relentlessly marketable. Knowledge is a form of hustle. You do not read to learn; you read to lead. You do not listen to understand; you listen to find an opening for your next contribution. American speech has become entrepreneurial: intellect that sells itself with a smile, charisma that disguises the absence of depth, confidence that compensates for the lack of actual knowledge. This is the cultural heart of The Monologue Society: where identity and attention are indistinguishable, and where to pause is to perish.

Travel east and you will find a different flavour entirely. In Warsaw, Prague, or Sofia, the monologue remains alive and well —but stripped of its Anglo-American sheen. Eastern Europe produces storytellers who carry the gravitas of centuries. They speak not to impress, but to endure. Their monologues are philosophical, weary, tinged with the melancholy of history. At a café in Kraków, a man might speak uninterrupted for twenty minutes about the futility of politics, the mediocrity of modern literature, and the moral decline of television presenters—all before his espresso cools. You listen not because he is right, but because he is magnificently wrong in an interesting way. There is a weight to his words, the residue of a history that has taught his people that certainty is a luxury they cannot afford. There is no need to "perform" intelligence here; only to possess it. The monologue in Eastern Europe is not a bid for attention but a form of survival. It is the voice of someone who has learned that the world rarely listens, so when they speak, they speak with the full force of their being, knowing that this might be their only opportunity to be heard.

In contrast, in Athens, Naples, or Barcelona, monologue is an art of passion, not philosophy. Every statement is a story. Every story is a confession. The monologue here is communal—it invites interruption, laughter, applause. It is not a speech but a shared song. The Greek grandparent and the Neapolitan taxi driver are united by the same conviction: that the most efficient way to deliver truth is loudly and with hand gestures. The Mediterranean monologue is less about winning an argument and more about creating an experience. It is theatre without a script, poetry without a page. If the Anglo-American monologue is a TED Talk, the Mediterranean one is a one-man opera. It is the sound of life being lived at full volume, with no apologies and no fear of taking up space.

And then there are the Nordics. Where the rest of us are trapped in our own soundtracks, they remain admirably resistant to the tyranny of the monologue. A Swede does not monologue. A Dane will tell a story only when asked, and even then it will be brief, factual, and suspiciously modest. They speak in sentences, not epics. Their power lies in proportion. When a Norwegian finishes speaking, you know the conversation is safe. You can breathe again. They are the antidote to Back to Me culture: proof that self-control can be a form of self-expression. Where others fill silence with noise, the Nordic speaker fills it with meaning. Their monologues, when they occur, are brief and devastating. A single sentence that contains more wisdom than an hour of American TED Talk rambling. They do not perform their thoughts; they think them, and then occasionally, if absolutely necessary, they share them. The Nordic monologue is a monologue that does not wish to be a monologue.

In much of East and Southeast Asia, the monologue takes a subtler form. Here, dominance is tempered by etiquette. People speak in turns, but the hierarchy within the conversation is often invisible to outsiders. In Japan or Korea, the senior voice is expected to fill the air—not out of vanity, but out of duty. The monologue becomes a performance of responsibility. The younger participants listen, nod, and occasionally interject to signal respect. It is dominance with decorum: an elegant dictatorship of speech. In China, meanwhile, public monologue has been nationalised. Long speeches from leaders are part of the cultural fabric—but so, too, are the quiet side conversations at the dinner table, where meaning is conveyed in what is not said. The Asian monologue is not self-promotion; it is choreography. Everyone knows the steps.

The Arab tradition preserves something the rest of us have lost—the monologue as a shared act of beauty. In the majlis, stories unfold like woven carpets. They are long, ornate, full of digressions, poetry, and metaphor. To speak well is to honour the listener. To listen well is to honour the speaker. The ego is there, yes, but refined by hospitality. It is a world where dominance is exercised not through interruption, but through generosity of language. A monologue in the Arab tradition is not someone grabbing the floor; it is someone offering a gift. The listener is invited into a world of words, images, and ideas. They emerge changed, enriched, honoured by what they have heard.

The Balkans deserve a category of their own—a unique blend of Slavic candour and Mediterranean intensity. Here, monologues are delivered with the force of personal testimony and the rhythm of comedy. People speak as if addressing both you and history at once. Every story is a protest, a poem, and a punchline. The listener nods, smokes, and occasionally interjects with a "You think that's bad?" before launching into their own chapter. It is chaos, but glorious chaos—conversation as catharsis. By the time the evening is over, you have heard enough stories to fill a novel, laughed enough to hurt, and felt somehow understood by people you have just met. The Balkan monologue is survival dressed up as entertainment.

Across cultures, the rise of The Monologue Society stems from the same root: fear. The fear of silence, of invisibility, of irrelevance. We talk endlessly because silence no longer feels safe. We fill every gap with ourselves—our achievements, our traumas, our take on last night's documentary. We confuse visibility with value. In a world where everyone is trying to "build their brand," the self has become the only reliable subject. Personal narrative is the currency of the age. But what we have lost in this process is something precious: the ability to think together. The capacity for ideas to emerge from dialogue rather than from monologue. The possibility that someone else's perspective might actually change us.

Social media is our global amphitheatre. The influencer's vlog, the CEO's LinkedIn sermon, the activist's 40-tweet thread—all belong to the same grand project: the performance of significance. Each post is a soliloquy, each reply a competing script. We are all protagonists now, wandering through an endless Shakespearean tragedy titled Everyone Else Is Wrong. And yet, buried beneath the irony, lies longing—the desire to be seen, heard, and remembered. We are not entirely cynical about this. We genuinely want connection. We genuinely believe that if we just speak loudly enough, clearly enough, convincingly enough, we will be understood. We will matter. We will finally be enough.

Interestingly, cultures are beginning to push back. In Japan, there is a resurgence of ma—the appreciation of space and silence in conversation. In Denmark, "hygge" has reclaimed intimacy over display. In Central Europe, a quiet intellectualism persists—cafés where people still debate poetry without filming it, still think without performing their thinking, still exist without broadcasting their existence. Even in the United States, the success of "quiet" podcasts and long-form interviews hints at fatigue with the perpetual shout. Perhaps the pendulum is swinging back. Perhaps the world is ready, once again, to hear itself think.

Every civilisation has its talkers, its interrupters, its natural broadcasters. But true conversation—that delicate equilibrium of speaking and listening—is humanity's oldest and rarest art. To recover it, we must learn from each other's rhythms. From the British, subtlety. From the Americans, enthusiasm. From the Eastern Europeans, honesty. From the Mediterraneans, warmth. From the Asians, restraint. From the Nordics, silence. If we could somehow combine them all, perhaps we would rediscover what conversation was meant to be: not a declaration, but an encounter. Not a performance, but a meeting of minds.

Until then, The Monologue Society will thrive—expanding across dinner tables, offices, and social feeds, humming the same universal refrain: Enough about you. Back to me. The soliloquy continues. The audience has left. And we keep talking, to a theatre that is increasingly empty, hoping that someone, somewhere, is still listening.

CHAPTER FOUR: THE "AS I WAS SAYING" SPECIES -THE ZOOLOGY OF THE CONVERSATIONAL DOMINATOR

The Animals of Ego

Every culture has its animals of ego. You can find them grazing at dinner parties, prowling in boardrooms, or holding court at conferences. They are the natural fauna of the modern world—creatures sustained entirely by attention, by the validation of strangers, by the constant reassurance that they matter. To study them is to study ourselves, because we all carry a little bit of them inside us. The challenge is not to eradicate them—they are part of the human condition—but to recognise them. To name them. To understand their motivations and their methods. And perhaps, most importantly, to avoid becoming one.

The One-Upper exists in every society. They are a conversational predator that feeds on your achievements and replaces them with their own. You mention you have just run a half marathon; they have just completed an ultramarathon blindfolded, in the Gobi Desert, for charity. You share that your child is learning French; theirs is fluent in Mandarin, Arabic, and quantum mechanics. You say you had a nice weekend; they describe a weekend so filled with adventure and accomplishment that your entire existence suddenly feels pallid by comparison. The British variant does this with quiet understatement: "Oh, I think we did something similar in Tuscany, terribly small vineyard, really." The American version is a full-throated sermon of self-improvement: "That's awesome! You know, when I ran my fifth Ironman…" In Eastern Europe, the One-Upper has evolved into something darker and more philosophical. They do not just outperform you; they out-suffer you. You have had a hard week? They have had a hard life, and they would be delighted to explain it to you, preferably over vodka, at length, with maximum detail.

The Data Dropper thrives in managerial habitats and technology conferences. They do not tell stories; they deploy statistics. Every point comes armed with data, graphs, and the phrase, "The research actually shows…" Their goal is not enlightenment but submission. They want you to concede, to accept their superior knowledge, to bow before the altar of their carefully researched facts. In Silicon Valley, they quote neuroscience and productivity hacks. In London, they cite The Economist and obscure economic theories. In Warsaw, they reference IMF reports and mention a vague cousin who works in Brussels and knows important people. Their natural enemy is the Storyteller, because facts can never compete with a good anecdote told at volume. Data does not evoke emotion. Statistics do not create connection. But a story—a well-told, emotionally resonant story—can override logic entirely. The Data Dropper knows this, which is why they are so committed to drowning out the storytellers with their superior facts.

The Humblebrag is perhaps the most evolved of all conversational species—a perfect fusion of arrogance and camouflage. They express pride disguised as pain. "Oh, I am exhausted. I have just flown back from the Maldives—too much scuba this week." The British pioneered this technique centuries ago. The class system demanded modesty while rewarding vanity. The result: generations of people who can boast without ever using a positive adjective. They have perfected the art of complaint-as-achievement. They have mastered the humble-sounding brag. The American version dropped the subtlety entirely. Their humblebrags are open self-promotion wrapped in inspirational language: "I am so humbled to be recognised as one of Forbes' 30 Under 30!" Translation: I am not humble at all. I am delighted. I am thrilled. I want you to know how successful I am. In Poland and Eastern Europe, the Humblebrag has a tragicomic twist. It often begins with complaint and ends in superiority: "It is awful, everyone keeps asking me to give interviews again." "I cannot go to the café anymore without being recognised." "It is a burden, really, having such a successful career."

The Name Dropper is perhaps the oldest conversational parasite in recorded history. Where others trade in ideas, the Name Dropper trades in proximity to fame. They do not need achievements of their own; they have contacts. They collect celebrity adjacency like currency—validation by osmosis. If they can convince you that they know someone famous, or have met someone important, or went to school with someone who went to school with someone who is now significant, they have somehow borrowed that person's importance and made it their own. The British version favours understatement: "I was chatting to Benedict the other night—terribly grounded chap." The implication is that they and Benedict Cumberbatch are intimates, which is almost certainly false, but the understatement makes it feel more believable. The American goes full volume: "So I was with Elon at South by Southwest, and he said—" (He almost certainly did not). The French elevate name-dropping to philosophy: "As Foucault once said to me —well, to all of us, in a lecture, but I felt it was to me." In Eastern Europe, it takes on an entirely different energy— pragmatic, transactional, and often hilarious. You mention your business idea; they mention their friend who once met a deputy minister who might still have a cousin in customs. The goal is not glamour; it is access. Name-dropping here is not vanity; it is survival. In Italy, of course, it is art. "Carlo, you know Carlo? No? He was the chef at the place where Sophia Loren used to go. Anyway…" Each name-drop is both an anecdote and an aria. But nowhere is the species more audacious than in the Balkans, where dropping names of local oligarchs or minor television personalities carries the same social wattage as citing Plato.

The Armchair Philosopher is an ancient breed—the self-anointed sage who sees every conversation as an opportunity to display the full weight of their intellect. They speak with the gravity of Plato and the certainty of someone who has skimmed a few articles on Medium. They are fluent in half-remembered Nietzsche and full-length TED Talks. They have read just enough to be dangerous, understood just enough to be insufferable. In France, they thrive in cafés, gesticulating with cigarettes and despair, speaking about the collapse of Western civilisation as if they have witnessed it personally. In Britain, they wear tweed and say "Quite" before dismantling your worldview. In Eastern Europe, they speak with existential melancholy: "Of course the West is collapsing, but it always collapses beautifully." They are the person who somehow manages to turn every conversation into a lecture, every discussion into a seminar where they are the only speaker worth listening to. Every culture loves them, and every dinner guest secretly dreads them.

The Serial Interrupter is a creature we have met in previous chapters, but the modern Serial Interrupter has adapted beautifully to globalisation. In New York, they interrupt for dominance. In Rome, for love. In London, to show they are engaged. In Sofia, because they have already guessed the ending and are impatient for you to catch up. Their defining trait is the inability to wait. They do not listen; they reload. They do not engage; they hijack. Their worst moment comes when faced with a Nordic listener—that serene, silent, unflappable wall of composure. The Serial Interrupter throws everything they have at it: words, jokes, anecdotes, personal revelations. The silence wins. It always does.

The Empathetic Hijacker is a newer species, emerging from therapy culture and the self-help internet. They appear compassionate—nodding, murmuring, saying "I totally understand"—until they pivot, stealthily, into their own story. You talk about your breakup; they talk about their divorce. You mention grief; they launch into a full monologue on healing. The shift is seamless, the empathy performative. In America, it is therapeutic. "Thank you for sharing that vulnerability with me. It reminds me of my journey." In Britain, it is politely suffocating. "Oh yes, quite awful. Reminds me of when I went through something terribly similar." In Central Europe, it is often mistaken for affection when actually it is just rudeness. And in Asia, it is nearly extinct—people there still understand the difference between listening and waiting to speak.

The Cultural Chameleon adapts its species depending on context. In a British boardroom, it performs modesty. In an American conference, it performs enthusiasm. In a Parisian salon, it performs intellect. In a Tokyo meeting, it performs respect. In a Brazilian bar, it performs warmth. Every society breeds its own hybrid species. The British Modest Alpha. The American Inspirational Over-Sharer. The Italian Anecdotal Philosopher. The Polish Tragic Humourist. The Scandinavian Stoic Minimalist. The Indian Metaphysical Networker. Each performs the same function—to keep the spotlight firmly where it belongs: on themselves. Together, they form the vast ecosystem of The "As I Was Saying" Species: those who believe conversation is merely an intermission between their own thoughts.

Why do we all do it? Why do we all occasionally become one of these species? Mock them as we might, these characters exist because they satisfy a deep psychological need—the need to be visible in a world that no longer listens. The name-dropper seeks validation. The humblebrag seeks reassurance. The one-upper seeks safety in superiority. The armchair philosopher seeks intellectual dominance. The serial interrupter—poor creature—simply cannot bear the fear of being forgotten. They are not monsters; they are mirrors. They reflect our own desperate need to matter, to be heard, to have our existence acknowledged.

QUENTIN DRUMMOND ANDERSON

The uncomfortable truth is that every one of us has a touch of the "As I Was Saying" species inside us. We have all dropped a name at an inopportune moment. We have all hijacked a story that was not ours. We have all mistaken performance for connection. We have all wanted so badly to be impressive that we sacrificed the possibility of being authentic. The key is not to silence the voice entirely—that voice exists for a reason, born of legitimate human need—but to learn when to step back from the microphone. Because in a world where everyone is shouting "Back to me!", the rarest and most magnetic thing you can say is: "Tell me more." That is the real power. That is what the species have not yet learned.

CHAPTER FIVE: ZOOM AND THE RISE OF THE TALKING HEAD - HOW THE WORLD LEARNED TO PERFORM FROM THE NECK UP

It's all techs fault

It began, as revolutions often do, with good intentions and bad Wi-Fi. When the pandemic struck in 2020, humanity retreated indoors—armed with webcams, ring lights, and the stubborn conviction that if we just kept talking, kept meeting, kept performing connection through screens, civilisation might somehow continue. And it did, sort of. We adapted. We learned to work from home. We figured out how to conduct meetings without being in the same room. We discovered that Zoom could substitute for the office, that video calls could replace handshakes, that pixels could somehow stand in for presence. But what also survived—and flourished, metastasising across our collective experience—was the global cult of the Talking Head. Within months, offices became studios. The conference call became theatre. And everyone, everywhere, learned the same unnerving truth: when the mute button is off, the ego is on. We all became performers. We all became broadcasters. We all became intimately aware of our own faces, our own lighting, our own presence on screen. And in that awareness, something shifted. Conversation changed. We changed.

Before 2020, our social lives were limited by geography. You could only have a conversation with the people in the room with you. You were constrained by distance, by time zones, by the simple logistics of human movement. Then, overnight, we were all invited to the same meeting—one vast, lagging, multicultural improv class called Zoom. The platform promised equality: everyone, regardless of rank or status, reduced to a tiny square on a screen. In practice, it became a perfect microcosm of global conversational behaviour—compressed, pixelated, and brutally exposed. The Italians waved. The Americans grinned. The British apologised for existing. The Japanese bowed slightly before their webcams. The Eastern Europeans stared impassively, wondering who wrote this script and why everyone was pretending to enjoy it. The Nordics said very little and left early.

In the United States, the Zoom revolution was met with pure evangelical enthusiasm. Meetings became motivational sermons. Every session began like a pep rally and ended like a therapy session. People spoke in soundbites and smiles, performing productivity with Broadway sincerity. The webcam was no longer a tool—it was a mirror, a stage, a branding opportunity. Americans perfected the Zoom persona: confident, engaged, permanently mid-gesture, forever nodding. Silence was treated like a system error. A pause in speech meant the connection had frozen. An unmuted moment of quiet meant something had gone wrong. So people filled the silence with enthusiasm. "Great to see you all! You are amazing! Let us crush this quarter!" Every line delivered with the intensity of someone trying to prove their worth through a screen. The Zoom background became a statement. The lighting became a commitment. The performance became the point.

In Britain, the adjustment was far less seamless. The national instinct for self-effacement collided violently with the demand to appear confident on camera. The average British Zoom call looked like a hostage video filmed in a study full of unpaid books. Participants muted themselves compulsively, spoke only when addressed, and began every sentence with "Sorry, just to say…"

The British apologised to the camera. They apologised to the meeting. They apologised to the very concept of visibility. When forced to make eye contact with the little glowing lens, they apologised again—to themselves, to their own reflection, to the universe for taking up pixels. For a nation that thrives on irony, the webcam offered none. You could see your own face reacting in real time—an existential crisis in 1080p. The forced intimacy of the video call horrified them. The demand to perform their presence while simultaneously appearing unbothered drove them to distraction. They adapted by being as minimal as possible. Shoulders from the neck down. No background. No attempt at staging. Just the raw, unbothered British face, looking faintly embarrassed to be there at all.

Across Eastern Europe, something remarkable happened. People who had spent decades perfecting their poker-faced resilience for bureaucratic meetings were suddenly in their element. While Western colleagues panicked about "virtual presence," the Poles, Czechs, and Romanians logged in, said exactly what needed to be said, and logged off. No small talk, no smiles, no slogans—just raw efficiency and a faint sense that everyone else was wasting electricity. The Eastern European Zoom manner was a revelation: direct, unfiltered, slightly terrifying. Where Americans said "Love your energy!" they said, "That is wrong." Where Brits said, "We might consider," they said, "We will not." To Western ears, it sounded rude. To them, it was liberation. The mask of corporate civility could finally be dropped. The Zoom screen somehow gave them permission to be honest.

In France, video meetings became miniature salons—everyone competing to be the most eloquent disembodied head. Participants spoke in paragraphs. Interruption was expected, encouraged, and occasionally applauded. The French treated the Zoom call as an intellectual amphitheatre. When connection lagged, they simply continued speaking, confident that the brilliance of their thought would transcend bandwidth limitations. If Descartes had been alive in 2020, he would have muted everyone else and announced, "I think, therefore I am —and I have the floor." The French understood intuitively that on Zoom, the person who speaks is the person who exists. The person who mutes themselves is, quite literally, invisible.

In Italy, Spain, and Greece, Zoom meetings became family reunions. Conversations overlapped joyously. People gestured off-screen. Children and grandparents drifted through frames like extras in a Fellini film. It was chaos—but it worked. Mediterranean cultures approached Zoom as if it were a dinner table that happened to exist on the internet. Why pause when you can participate? To Mediterraneans, the idea of taking turns felt unnatural. Conversation was meant to be simultaneous, overlapping, full of warmth and noise. Meetings were symphonies of simultaneous speech, with each participant convinced the others were listening. And, in their way, they were.

The Nordic approach to Zoom was the opposite: beautiful, silent landscapes punctuated by the occasional "Yes." Participants appeared in immaculate lighting, spoke once, and disappeared again, leaving everyone unsure whether they had been real or AI. Their restraint was unnerving but oddly comforting— a reminder that silence still had meaning. While others fought for airtime, they conserved it like natural resource. When asked for feedback, a Swede might simply nod. That nod carried the weight of an entire PowerPoint presentation.

In the Middle East, Zoom meetings took on the spirit of the majlis. The host greeted everyone warmly, camera perfectly framed, often with a coffee cup in hand. Meetings began not with agendas but with blessings. It was interruption as generosity—the same social rhythm transposed into pixels. Even online, conversation remained an art of respect, warmth, and timing. While Westerners tried to "stick to the schedule," their Middle Eastern counterparts stuck to tradition: make people feel seen before being heard.

In Asia, online communication adopted the same careful hierarchies as real-world interaction. No one spoke out of turn. Titles were observed. Even virtual bowing became a thing—tiny dips of the head visible on camera. Meetings were smooth, polite, and slightly surreal: a choreography of respect performed across fibre-optic lines. If someone did interrupt, it was done so gently that it felt like an apology wrapped in grammar. And when Western colleagues filled silences with nervous chatter, the Asian participants simply waited, smiling, until the noise subsided—proof that patience still trumps pixels.

What united everyone—whether loud or restrained, expressive or stoic—was the camera. It turned us all into performers, conscious of our image, our lighting, our "presence." We began to speak not to each other, but to our own reflections. The result was a kind of collective narcissism disguised as collaboration. Every meeting became a competition for eye contact and airtime. The mute button turned into a moral test: who had the discipline to use it? The video call became a tool not just for communication, but for performance evaluation. Are they engaged? Are they paying attention? Can we see them? And if we cannot see them, do they still exist?

There emerged a new species of professional: the Mute Master. Those who could remain silent for an entire meeting, faces unreadable, unmuting only once to deliver a single, devastatingly concise insight. The British envied them, the Americans admired them, and the Eastern Europeans quietly recognised their own. They had discovered something radical: that in a world addicted to self-broadcast, restraint is rebellion.

As the pandemic dragged on and video calls multiplied, the world seemed to forget how to listen. Webinars replaced dialogues, panels became echo chambers, and podcasts multiplied like mushrooms after rain. Everyone had something to say—and, conveniently, a microphone. The line between "work" and "performance" dissolved entirely. We were all talking heads now. We were all broadcasting. We were all trying to be heard from tiny squares on screens.

By the time offices reopened, the habits had taken root. People interrupted more, listened less, and mistook visibility for participation. The Zoom era had trained us to believe that being seen was the same as being heard. Meetings in London felt more American. Meetings in New York felt more Italian. Meetings in Warsaw felt more decisive than ever. Globalisation had achieved what centuries of diplomacy never could: a single, shared conversational language—noise.

The cultural aftermath lingers. We learned that under pressure, we all default to our cultural type. The British become more apologetic. The Americans more enthusiastic. The French more eloquent. The Eastern Europeans more blunt. The Nordic more silent. But we also learned something else: that distance sometimes clarifies conversation. That a screen can feel safer than a room. That pixels can substitute for presence—imperfectly, but sufficiently. And perhaps most importantly, we learned that the real power in any conversation is not in being visible, but in being heard. Not in speaking, but in understanding. Not in the performance, but in the connection beneath it.

If the 20th century was the Age of the Microphone, the 21st is the Age of the Webcam. We have all learned to perform from the neck up. We have all discovered our best angles, our best lighting, our best "Zoom faces." We have all become intimately aware of the gap between how we think we appear and how we actually appear. And in that awareness lies both horror and opportunity. Horror because we cannot escape the performance. Opportunity because, finally, we might be ready to ask: is this really how we want to communicate? Is visibility the same as connection? Is being on camera the same as being present?

The answers, whispered through glitchy audio and frozen screens, might finally be: no. And perhaps, just perhaps, that realisation might be the beginning of something better.

CHAPTER SIX: EGO IN HD- HOW THE WORLD FELL IN LOVE WITH ITS OWN REFLECTION

Take a Picture

The smartphone camera did not merely change how we see the world. It fundamentally altered how the world sees us. It changed our sense of self. It changed our relationship to truth. It changed the very nature of existence itself. Once upon a time, you needed a film crew, a studio, lighting equipment, and at least a hint of celebrity to be famous. You needed gatekeepers. You needed permission. You needed to be selected by those in power to have your image broadcast to the world. Now, all you need is an angle, a filter, and a decent Wi-Fi signal. You need nothing but the willingness to be seen. The result is the most powerful global ideology since capitalism: visibility. We no longer think, "I post therefore I am." We think, more desperately, "I am only when I post." If your life is not documented, photographed, filtered, captioned, and shared, did it really happen? If no one saw you living it, did you actually live it? The smartphone has made philosophers of us all—but philosophers obsessed with a single question: How do I look?

Every civilisation once had its own mirror. For the ancient Greeks, it was the theatre—a place where you could see yourself reflected in the reactions of an audience. For the French, it was the café—a stage where ideas were performed and identity was constructed. For the British, it was the dinner table—a theatre of manners where social position was continually reinforced. For

Americans, it was the frontier—that mythical space where you could reinvent yourself, be anyone you wanted to be. Now, for all of us, it is the front-facing camera. Democratically available to anyone with a smartphone. Infinitely flattering thanks to filters and strategic angles. Mercilessly addictive because it rewards you with likes, comments, shares. Every tap of the selfie lens says the same thing: "Back to me." Every filtered photograph is a small act of narcissism, but also a small act of defiance. Look at me. Notice me. Validate me. Prove that I exist.

In the United States, self-expression has long been a birthright —enshrined in law, celebrated in culture, encouraged from childhood. From Walt Whitman's Song of Myself to Oprah's couch to the rise of the influencer economy, the national creed has been simple and consistent: tell your story, loudly, and do not apologize for it. Social media merely industrialised what was already there. Instagram became the church of confidence; TikTok, its choir. YouTube became the temple of the self-made celebrity. To be modest is to be invisible; to be visible is to be relevant. The American influencer speaks like a preacher—earnest, smiling, forever on the brink of revelation. "Guys, I just wanted to share something super vulnerable today," they announce, before revealing something that is not vulnerable at all but rather a carefully calculated performance of vulnerability. It is confession as content, therapy as marketing, the personal repackaged as universal wisdom. The American self on social media is a brand. It is something to be managed, cultivated, monetised. Your authenticity is your selling point. Your trauma is your content. Your life is your business model.

Britain's relationship with self-display is more conflicted, more tortured. A nation raised on understatement suddenly found itself thrust under ring lights, forced to perform for algorithms, required to participate in the global ego economy or risk irrelevance. British influencers mastered the art of self-deprecation as performance: "Can't believe I am posting this, absolutely mortified—anyway, here is me looking fabulous." It is modesty with lighting design. It is humility as branding. The stiff upper lip has become the soft glow of a selfie ring. Meanwhile, intellectual life has followed suit. Even the most serious pundits now film themselves explaining geopolitics in their kitchens, standing in front of bookshelves meant to signal intelligence, performing thought in real time for an invisible audience. The British have learned to perform confidence while maintaining plausible deniability about the performance.

In France, self-expression remains elegant, ironic, and beautifully self-aware. Instagram feeds are curated like gallery walls—more mood than message. A French influencer does not say, "Look at me." They say, "Behold, the concept of me." They post an espresso, a quotation from Camus, a sigh. The lighting is always perfect. The composition is always thoughtful. The message is always subtle. It is ego expressed through aesthetic refinement rather than direct proclamation. "Therefore I pose, therefore I am," the French Instagram feed seems to say. There is something almost philosophical about French narcissism on social media. They are not trying to be liked; they are trying to be appreciated as a work of art.

For Eastern Europe, the selfie revolution arrived as a strange kind of freedom. After decades of censorship and conformity, self-presentation felt like rebellion. But the region's relationship with pride is complicated. The Polish entrepreneur posts success with a mixture of triumph and apology. The Ukrainian artist documents resilience and ruin side by side. The Romanian influencer blends glamour with grit, oscillating between couture and cynicism. The result is a social-media aesthetic best described as melancholy fabulous—a cocktail of confidence and disbelief that anyone is watching. There is an irony running through Eastern European Instagram that you do not find elsewhere. We survived history; we can survive hashtags. The ego on display is both assertive and apologetic, both proud and skeptical. It is the voice of people who have learned not to trust appearances, including their own.

In Scandinavia, where humility is almost constitutional, overt self-promotion is frowned upon. Yet even there, the mirror beckoned. The Nordic influencer's feed is austere: a forest, a candle, a perfect cup of coffee. The message is clear—I am calm, therefore I exist. Their ego is expressed through restraint. Where others shout, they whisper—and somehow get twice as many likes. The Scandinavian Instagram aesthetic is one of quiet confidence, of beauty that does not need to announce itself. There is something almost rebellious about their refusal to perform desperation for attention. By refusing to play the game, they somehow win it.

In Italy, Spain, and Greece, the camera simply formalised what was already true: life is a performance, and the self is the greatest performance of all. Self-expression is not vanity; it is vitality. The Italian Instagram is an opera: family, fashion, food, gesture. The Spanish is pure warmth—endless gatherings, the world as one long Sunday lunch. The Greek is philosophy in sunlight: selfies on ruins, history as backdrop, tragedy and tan lines intertwined. Here, ego is not arrogance. It is joy. It is the sound of life being lived at full volume, unapologetically, gloriously.

In the Middle East, social media became both a platform and a paradox. On one hand, it offered freedom of voice and image in cultures where such freedom was historically restricted. On the other hand, it collided with traditions of modesty and privacy. The result is a fascinating fusion—elegance wrapped in discretion. The influencer may wear couture, but her captions speak of faith, gratitude, and family. The male counterpart might pose beside a Lamborghini, but the comment will read: "Alhamdulillah"—praise be to God. It is the fusion of humility and high definition—reverence expressed through resolution. The ego on display is always contextualized within something larger than the self.

Asia turned self-presentation into both art and science. In South

Korea, beauty filters are national infrastructure—so prevalent that people have begun to look like their filtered versions. In China, livestreaming is a billion-dollar economy where young people perform their lives in real time for virtual audiences. In Japan, the cult of kawaii (cuteness) merged with a Zen-like obsession for perfection creates a strange alchemy. But the cultural paradox remains: the same societies that value modesty in person have built digital worlds of flawless projection. The Chinese influencer may be meticulously styled, but her caption will quote Confucius. The Japanese salaryman, shy in meetings, becomes a vlogger by night. The Thai student poses mid-laugh, tagging friends with the universal caption: "Just fun." In Asia, ego is not rebellion; it is refinement—the art of harmony through curation.

Across Africa and Latin America, social media is not a mirror of insecurity but of celebration. Nigerian influencers exude entrepreneurial flair; Brazilian creators turn everyday life into carnival. Here, visibility is empowerment—the long-overdue correction to centuries of misrepresentation. When a Lagos designer posts a photo in neon colours, it is not vanity; it is a manifesto. When a Colombian musician uploads a street performance, it is joy as resistance. Ego here is not individualism; it is collective pride. The self on display represents not just the individual but the culture, the community, the identity that has been historically silenced.

What unites this global spectacle of self-display is the machine beneath it. Algorithms reward outrage, confidence, and beauty —the three great currencies of the digital ego. Silence, subtlety, and humility are punished by obscurity. We have built a world where the invisible might as well not exist. If you are not online, you are not alive—or so the feed insists. The algorithm does not care about your inner life. It cares about engagement. It cares about whether you will scroll, click, comment, share. It cares about whether your image will provoke a reaction. So we optimise for reactions. We curate for engagement. We perform for algorithms. We have outsourced the evaluation of our worth to machines that do not understand meaning, only metrics.

The psychological cost of all this ego in high definition is staggering. The endless loop of self-presentation has made the ego fragile, addicted to validation yet terrified of irrelevance. Across cultures, anxiety now speaks the same language: the Japanese hikikomori retreating from digital life; the American teenager refreshing notifications obsessively; the Polish entrepreneur watching likes dip after a serious post; the British journalist deleting tweets at midnight in a panic. Different contexts, same craving: attention as proof of existence. The fear is universal: if I am not being seen, I am not real.

And yet, everywhere, resistance stirs. In Japan, the rise of "no-filter" movements. In Italy, influencers turning their phones off for Lent. In Poland, campaigns celebrating normalność—normality—as beauty. In Scandinavia, "digital detox" is now a status symbol. Even in the United States, the new luxury is privacy. The most expensive thing you can own is now the absence of your own image online. There is something almost rebellious about refusing to perform, about stepping back from the mirror, about allowing yourself to exist without documentation.

The truth is that ego has always existed. People have always wanted to be seen, to matter, to leave a mark. What changed is the resolution. We can now zoom in on ourselves until there is nothing left to see but pixels and filters and curated fragments of a life that may or may not be real. But across the world—from Tokyo to Turin, Lagos to Los Angeles—the same truth endures: when everyone is broadcasting, the most radical act is authenticity. Not the curated kind, not the branded vulnerability, but the quiet, unfiltered moment when the lens is off and the conversation turns outward. Because in a world lit by ring lights, the rarest illumination is still human. It is still presence. It is still the moment when someone looks at you—

really looks at you, not at your image—and sees you.

That moment is becoming increasingly rare. But perhaps that is precisely why it matters so much.

CHAPTER SEVEN: THE EMPATHY MIRAGE -WHY LISTENING HAS BECOME PERFORMANCE ART

Blah,blah,blah

There is a paradox at the heart of modern communication. We have never had more language for empathy, yet we have never been worse at actually empathising. We speak constantly of "listening," of "making space," of "holding space," of "validating feelings." We perform these acts with theatrical sincerity. We attend workshops on active listening. We read self-help books about emotional intelligence. We post supportive comments on social media. We say "I hear you" with the intensity of someone who absolutely does not hear you but wants very badly for you to believe that they do. Empathy has become a performance, a skill to be learned and demonstrated, rather than a genuine state of being with another person. It has become, in short, another form of Back to Me.

The phenomenon is global but the presentation is culturally specific. In America, empathy is technicolor and enthusiastic. The empathetic American says, "I totally get it!" while already thinking about how your experience relates to theirs. They nod with exaggerated understanding. They lean forward. They make eye contact. Their entire body language screams: I am listening! Which, paradoxically, proves that they are not. Real listening requires invisibility. It requires the listener to step back, not forward. It requires restraint, not display. But American culture has transformed empathy into a performance of attentiveness, a way of signalling moral superiority through demonstrable concern. The empathetic American wants you to know they are empathetic. They want to be seen as compassionate, as evolved, as emotionally intelligent. But their empathy is ego in different clothing. It is narcissism wearing a therapist's voice.

In Britain, empathy takes a more muted, more sinister form. The British listener says, "Oh, how dreadfully difficult," while maintaining complete emotional distance. They offer tea. They maintain a safe conversational perimeter. Their empathy is expressed through propriety—the careful observation of social convention that somehow substitutes for actual feeling. The British have perfected the art of seeming to care while actually caring about seeming to care. It is empathy as manners, as the correct response to the correct emotional stimulus. But there is something almost cruel about it—the precision with which they perform sympathy without ever allowing genuine feeling to disturb the surface. The empathetic Brit never really opens. They never really meet you. They listen politely and then go back to their life, their feelings perfectly preserved in aspic, untouched by your vulnerability.

In France, empathy is philosophical and somewhat detached. The French listener nods thoughtfully while already constructing an intellectual response. They are considering your experience not as a human encounter but as a data point in a larger argument. Your suffering becomes material for their insight. Your vulnerability becomes an example for their theory. They say, "Yes, but one could argue," which is their way of transforming your lived experience into an abstract principle. It is empathy filtered through intellectualism—and something crucial is lost in translation. The French have convinced themselves that understanding something theoretically is the same as understanding it humanly. It is not.

In Eastern Europe, empathy is darker, more ironic. The Eastern European listener has often survived things your culture does not discuss at polite dinners. They have learned to listen without flinching, to absorb other people's pain without adding their own commentary. Their empathy is born from history—the understanding that suffering is universal and commentary is often useless. They listen quietly, sometimes nodding, sometimes lighting a cigarette and staring into the middle distance. When they do speak, it is often to say something devastating in its honesty: "Yes. Life is terrible." It is empathy as brutal acknowledgment. It does not comfort, but it does something perhaps more important: it stops pretending that comfort is possible. It meets suffering with the only honest response: recognition.

In Scandinavia, empathy is restrained to the point of seeming cold. A Swede listens without reaction. A Finn listens without speaking. A Norwegian listens with the patience of someone who understands that time is the only genuine response to pain. Their empathy is not performative; it is simply present. They do not need to demonstrate understanding. The fact that they are there, that they have not left, that they are still listening—that is enough. It is a revolutionary form of empathy in a world where everyone needs to be seen as empathetic. The Scandinavian does not care if you know they are listening. They are just listening. And somehow, that restraint speaks louder than all the nodding and affirming and therapeutic reframing in the world.

In the Mediterranean—Italy, Spain, Greece—empathy is immediate and emotional. The Mediterranean listener does not maintain distance; they collapse into your story, they adopt your pain, they make it theirs. They interrupt to say, "Oh no! That is terrible! Let me tell you something similar!" which sounds like hijacking but is actually a form of connection. The Mediterranean does not listen to understand; they listen to join. It is empathy as participation, as the erasure of the boundary between your experience and theirs. It is warm and chaotic and occasionally counterproductive, but it comes from a genuine place: the belief that suffering is best met with community, with the presence of others in the room, with the refusal to let anyone suffer alone. It is not always what you need, but it is always what they mean.

In Asia, empathy is hierarchical and contextual. You do not empathise with someone above you in the hierarchy; you respect them. You empathise with those below you, or with those in your peer group. Your empathy depends on understanding your position relative to theirs. In Japan, it is expressed through tiny adjustments—a bowed head, a respectful pause, the acknowledgment of someone else's suffering without the inappropriate familiarity of saying you understand it. In China, empathy is often expressed through action rather than words—someone brings food, someone provides practical help, someone sits with you. In India, empathy is woven into spirituality—the understanding that suffering is universal because rebirth is universal, and we have all suffered in all our lives. The empathetic response is not to fix the suffering but to contextualise it within something larger.

In the Middle East, empathy is expressed through hospitality and storytelling. The empathetic Arab does not interrogate your pain; they invite you to share it over tea, over time, in a space designed for such sharing. They listen not to solve but to witness. They understand that sometimes what people need is simply to be heard by someone who has nowhere else to be. There is no rush. There is no performance. There is just the majlis—the gathering—and the understanding that suffering is best met with presence and time and the willingness to sit with discomfort.

In Africa and Latin America, empathy is often collective and often tied to history. A Nigerian listens with the knowledge that colonialism happened. A South African listens with the memory of apartheid. A Colombian listens with the understanding that violence is not abstract. Their empathy comes loaded with context. It is not individual psychology; it is communal history.

When they listen to your pain, they are listening to it not as an isolated incident but as part of a larger pattern of human suffering. It is empathy that refuses to ignore systemic injustice. It is empathy as resistance.

What all these different cultural approaches to empathy share is this: the moment you perform empathy, you lose it. The moment you think about how to seem empathetic, you are no longer actually empathetic. You are performing empathy, which is entirely different. Performed empathy says: Look at how good a person I am. It is narcissism in a compassionate disguise. Real empathy is invisible. It requires you to step entirely out of the picture. It requires you to focus so completely on another person that you forget to think about how you are being perceived. It requires a kind of death of the self—a temporary erasure of your own needs, your own story, your own desire to be seen as a good listener.

But this is precisely what modern culture makes impossible. The rise of social media has militarised empathy. You are now expected to perform your empathy publicly. When someone experiences tragedy, the empathetic response is to post about it, to share your feelings, to make your caring visible to an audience. The result is a strange perversion of empathy—empathy as personal branding. I am a person who cares. I am a person who listens. I am a person who understands. Look at how much I care. You can see it in my comments. You can measure it in my engagement. The algorithms reward empathetic performance. The more visible your empathy, the more likes it generates. The more likes, the more real it seems.

Television and podcasts have created a new empathy economy. Professional listeners—therapists on YouTube, life coaches on Instagram, advice columnists on TikTok—now dispense empathy at scale. It is empathy industrialised, standardised, optimised for engagement. These professional empaths have learned that empathy generates loyalty. If I can make you feel heard, you will come back. You will subscribe. You will share my content. You will make me famous. The result is empathy as content creation, as a business model, as a way of accumulating followers. The professional empath becomes powerful not because they actually help anyone but because they perform the act of helping so convincingly that people believe they have been helped.

In workplaces, empathy has become a managerial tool. Companies invest in "emotional intelligence" training. They send managers to seminars to learn how to listen. The goal is not genuine connection—it is improved productivity, reduced turnover, optimised morale. Empathy becomes another metric, another KPI to track. The manager learns to say the right things at the right time: "I understand this is difficult. I hear your concern." It is empathy as technique, empathy as management strategy. It extracts the genuine care from empathy and leaves only the shell—the right words, the right tone, the right performance of understanding.

The psychology of this is worth examining. When you perform empathy, you often begin to believe your own performance. You think: I am a caring person because I say caring things. You mistake articulation for understanding. You confuse the words you say about empathy with the actual state of empathising. You become convinced that by using the correct language, by demonstrating the correct posture, by performing the correct emotional response, you have actually empathised. But empathy is not something you do. It is something you are, temporarily, when you forget about yourself entirely.

The result of all this performed empathy is a world that feels simultaneously more connected and more lonely. We have more language for connection than ever before. We are constantly being told that people care. We see endless expressions of solidarity and sympathy and support flowing across our screens. And yet we feel, with increasing desperation, that no one is actually listening. No one is actually seeing us. No one is actually present. Because they are all too busy performing the act of being present. They are all too concerned with how their presence appears. They are all too invested in being seen as empathetic to actually empathise.

There is a kind of empathy hunger spreading across the world. People are desperate to be truly heard—not performed at, not managed, not responded to with the correct therapeutic language, but genuinely, vulnerably heard. They want to be seen by someone who is not thinking about their own response. They want to matter to someone who is not concerned with how their mattering looks. They want to be listened to by someone who is not already constructing their own story to superimpose over what is being said. This hunger is visible everywhere: in the popularity of long-form interviews, in the rise of small support groups, in the demand for genuine human connection that cannot be algorithmically optimised.

The greatest act of empathy in the modern world is the simple act of not performing empathy. It is the decision to listen without needing to demonstrate that you are listening. It is the choice to let someone else be the centre of attention without immediately claiming some of that attention for yourself. It is the willingness to hear something difficult and not immediately transform it into a story about yourself. It is the radical act of stepping entirely out of the picture.

But this kind of empathy is not rewarded. It generates no followers. It cannot be turned into content. It offers no personal branding opportunity. It cannot be measured or quantified or optimised. It simply is—a moment of genuine human connection in a world addicted to the performance of connection. And yet, this is the empathy that heals. This is the empathy that changes people. This is the empathy that saves lives. Not the empathy that is seen, but the empathy that is felt. Not the empathy that is performed, but the empathy that is lived. Not the empathy that says "Back to Me" through the language of caring, but the empathy that says "It is all about you right now" and means it completely

CHAPTER EIGHT : THE PSYCHOLOGY OF THE UNHEARD

Insecurity, Attachment and the Need to Speak

At first glance, the conversational narcissist appears supremely confident. They fill the room with sound, stride verbally across topics, and seem utterly untroubled by self-doubt. Yet behind that fluency lies a deep unease — a fear of being unseen, unheard, and therefore unreal. The loudest talkers are not always the most secure; often they are simply the most frightened of silence.

Human beings are herd animals who long ago replaced fur and claws with conversation. To speak is to signal belonging. From infancy, the brain's limbic system registers responsiveness as safety. When a baby coos and a parent answers, the circuits governing attachment — the amygdala, insula and anterior cingulate cortex — record a vital lesson: sound brings connection. Silence, by contrast, feels like danger. Neuroscientists have shown that social exclusion activates the same pain networks as physical injury. In MRI scans, the dorsal anterior cingulate lights up when we are ignored or interrupted. That flicker of hurt, though invisible to others, can be powerful enough to shape an entire personality. The chronic interrupter, the compulsive sharer, the monologue artist — each may be driven by a subtle neurological craving: to re-establish connection by flooding the air with proof of presence.

In conversation, dopamine becomes the brain's currency of belonging. A nod of approval, a laugh, even the flicker of a notification — each delivers a small chemical reward. Modern life, engineered around constant feedback loops, has turned that dopamine trickle into a torrent. We speak to keep the flow going, mistaking momentary stimulation for emotional safety.

Attachment theory, developed by John Bowlby and Mary Ainsworth, offers another lens. The securely attached person can tolerate pauses, disagreement and not being the centre of attention. The anxiously attached cannot. For them, silence feels like abandonment; a pause in conversation is a small rehearsal of loss. Their words become a form of vigilance. They tell stories, reveal feelings prematurely and dominate the space not to impress but to prevent disconnection. They talk in order not to disappear.

Avoidant personalities, on the other hand, cloak their fear of intimacy behind detachment. They are the crisp, ironic conversationalists who intellectualise every subject, steering talk away from emotion. They appear self-contained, but their distance is another form of control — protection from the unpredictable demands of genuine exchange. Others oscillate between these extremes. Those who grew up amid inconsistency or trauma often reproduce that instability in speech: sudden oversharing followed by retreat, humour used as camouflage, erratic shifts of tone. Their conversations carry the emotional weather of their past.

Talking, in all these cases, offers an illusion of control over the unpredictable world of feeling. The more anxious the era, the greater the temptation to dominate the airwaves. During periods of collective uncertainty — financial crises, political turmoil, pandemics — verbal volume rises. When we cannot control events, we control the conversation about them. Digital media magnifies this urge. Typing, posting, or speaking into a camera offers a brief sense of mastery. Words become a way of keeping chaos at bay. To pause would be to feel powerless, and powerlessness is the one condition the modern ego cannot endure.

Listening, by contrast, requires surrender. Neuroscience shows that when we listen attentively, the brain's default mode network — the region responsible for self-referential thought — quietens. The listener's mind literally hushes its own narrative to make space for another's. For the chronic talker, that quiet feels threatening. Their brain, accustomed to the constant hum of self, treats silence as absence. To stop speaking is to risk vanishing.

Meditation research provides a fascinating counterpoint. Practices that train the mind to rest within silence increase grey-matter density in the prefrontal cortex and insula — areas linked to empathy and emotional regulation. In short, those who can bear silence reshape their brains towards compassion; those who cannot remain locked in self-defence.

Many conversational narcissists are, paradoxically, socially anxious. Eloquence becomes armour. The continuous monologue is a pre-emptive strike against humiliation: if they hold the stage, they cannot be rejected. Studies at University College London show that socially anxious individuals display heightened amygdala activity when anticipating judgment. Speech acts as a sedative — control through performance. The tragedy is that corporate culture now rewards this pathology. We have turned incessant articulation into a moral virtue. "Speaking up" has replaced thinking deeply. The extrovert ideal — polished, articulate, relentlessly "on message" — conceals what is essentially a socially rewarded anxiety disorder. The workplace talker is not always confident; they are often merely fluent at concealing fear.

Beneath these social adaptations lies something older and more painful: the trauma of being unheard. Psychotherapists speak of the "narcissistic wound" — early experiences of not being recognised or valued. These wounds can harden into lifelong patterns of self-assertion so constant they border on compulsion. Each story told, each interruption, each forced laugh is a plea: *Can you see me now?* But attention seized through dominance never feels safe. The talker must repeat the performance endlessly, mistaking fleeting notice for connection. The louder they speak, the emptier they feel.

Technology has industrialised this cycle. Social media functions as an external limbic system — measuring attention, rewarding visibility, punishing silence. Every "like" is a pellet of dopamine in the digital cage. Each post is a miniature experiment in attachment: will they respond? Will I exist? Neuroscientist Anna Lembke calls this the dopamine economy, a marketplace in which every ping resets our appetite for validation. Conversation itself begins to mimic this rhythm — shorter pauses, quicker replies, fewer genuine exchanges. We talk not to understand but to harvest micro-rewards of affirmation.

Gendered expectations shape these insecurities further. Men, raised to equate speech with authority, use words as proof of dominance; women, conditioned to nurture, use them as evidence of empathy. One fears irrelevance, the other invisibility. Both respond to cultural anxiety rather than innate difference. The result is a duet of overcompensation — one speaking to command, the other to connect, both terrified of the quiet that might reveal uncertainty.

Listening well requires a very different kind of courage. To be silent while another speaks demands the conviction that you will not vanish when your voice stops. It is an act of faith in one's own existence. Good listeners are not passive; they are secure. They hold the space with composure, confident that attention is not a commodity that must be seized. This is why the best therapists, mediators and leaders often say little. Their power lies not in speaking first but in absorbing fully.

Psychologically and neurologically, we are capable of learning this discipline. The prefrontal cortex — the brain's centre for reflection and restraint — can override the amygdala's impulsive need for validation. Simple habits help: breathing before replying, counting to three, letting the other person's final words linger before answering. Each pause recruits the neural circuits of empathy. Civility, then, is not mere etiquette; it is executive function — the regulation of one's own emotional hunger to make room for another's truth.

Imagine a culture that prized attentiveness as highly as articulation; a generation of children taught not only to "find their voice" but also to cherish their ears. Picture boardrooms where pauses signified respect, not hesitation. Such a shift would begin not with technology but with tolerance — the willingness to endure the mild anxiety of quiet without filling it with noise. Neuroscience already suggests the benefits. Silence lowers cortisol, steadies heart rate and enhances memory consolidation. Quiet minds recall more. A silent civilisation might even become a wiser one.

Ultimately, the tragedy of the talker is not arrogance but fragility. Their noise conceals longing. True empathy begins when the self can tolerate being momentarily irrelevant. Listening becomes liberation — the end of the exhausting need to prove existence through speech. Psychologists call the transformation *earned security*: the process of outgrowing anxious attachment through reliable, reciprocal connection. It begins with one simple act — letting someone else finish their sentence.

If *Back to Me* argues for anything, it is for the rehabilitation of the pause: that small, easily overlooked space between one person's thought and another's response. Neurologically, it is when our mirror neurons fire most strongly, aligning our emotional states. Morally, it is when our humanity re-enters the room. The silence we fear is not emptiness; it is the soil in which meaning grows.

CHAPTER NINE: LOUD MEN, LOUD WOMEN, AND THE MYTH OF BALANCE

Genders Redefined

For centuries, the world has been a duet in which one singer held the microphone and the other provided harmony. Now both are singing lead, often simultaneously, at considerable volume. The result is thrilling, chaotic, occasionally beautiful, and frequently exhausting. We have reached a peculiar moment in human history where the fundamental rules governing speech have shifted beneath our feet, creating terrain that is navigable but fundamentally unsettled.

The conversation about conversation becomes infinitely more complex when gender enters the equation. We inhabit an age where the traits rewarded in male speakers are routinely penalised in female ones, a double standard so persistent it has become almost invisible. A man who speaks assertively is celebrated as "decisive." A woman delivering identical words in identical tone is branded "intense," or more pejoratively, "shrill." It is the oldest inequality in auditory form, persisting everywhere from the conference room to the parliament to the dinner table where enlightened people congratulate themselves on their progressiveness whilst perpetuating the very hierarchies they believe they have transcended.

We tell girls to "find their voice"—a metaphor so ubiquitous it has calcified into wisdom. Schools dedicate assemblies to it.

Self-help books celebrate it. Well-meaning parents encourage it. Yet the moment that voice emerges at volume, society pivots into critique. We critique its tone, its pitch, its frequency, its assertiveness. Where were these caveats when we were encouraging them to speak up? The answer reveals an uncomfortable truth: we wanted them to have a voice, just not one that would genuinely challenge the existing power structure. We wanted their voice to be quieter than the men's, more decorative, more apologetic. We wanted them to occupy conversational space in a way that did not inconvenience those already comfortable there, those who had spent centuries believing that comfort was natural rather than constructed.

The American approach to gendered speech reveals itself most clearly in the boardroom. In the United States, conversation has always been framed as a form of competition, a straightforward extension of the American ethos of rugged individualism. This translates directly into conversational style: short, declarative sentences; relentless optimism; the conviction that ambiguity is weakness and hedging is intellectual dishonesty. American men learn early that loudness correlates with leadership, that volume is a form of credibility. Walk into any American corporate space and observe the dynamics. The dominance of physical and vocal space correlates not always with actual competence but with confidence, and confidence is a product dispensed far more liberally to men than women.

Women entering these same spaces have learned, through painful experience, to adjust their vocal patterns. They lower their pitch to avoid accusations of shrillness. They accelerate their pace to reduce the likelihood of being interrupted. They deploy strategic smiles to soften assertions that might otherwise be perceived as hostile or aggressive. They have become acoustic contortionists, bending their natural voice into shapes that will be palatable to existing power structures. Many succeed brilliantly within these constraints, but the effort required is visible to anyone paying close attention. They are running a marathon whilst simultaneously carrying an etiquette manual, navigating an obstacle course that men do not have to acknowledge, let alone navigate.

A new archetype has emerged in recent years: the Empowered Interruptor. She begins sentences with the apologetic "Sorry, but..." and concludes them with the self-diminishing "Does that make sense?"—linguistic armour so pervasive it has become nearly invisible. These are the conversational markers of someone who has learned to occupy space that was not architecturally designed for her, speaking in a frequency carefully calibrated not to threaten but gently to request permission. Even her empowerment must be apologised for, hedged, made acceptable to those who were comfortable before she arrived.

Britain's approach to gendered speech is more subtle but no less problematic in its outcomes. British conversation, as we have discussed extensively, runs on hierarchy disguised as politeness. The entire system was constructed in an era when women were either absent from formal discourse or expected to remain silent, and the infrastructure has never been properly renovated despite centuries of social change. Men still dominate through what might be called the gentle override—the interruption disguised as clarification. "Ah yes, that's an interesting point. But what you're really saying is..." The woman in such a space finds herself occupying deeply uncomfortable territory. Too loud and she becomes "aggressive" or "shrill." Too quiet and she is "uncertain" or "lacking confidence." There is no Goldilocks zone, no correct volume at which a woman can speak and be heard as simply, neutrally competent.

The classic British female response has been to play defence. She learns to listen with exceptional attentiveness. She becomes expert at summarising others' points. She is the one who rescues discussions that have gone off the rails, who steers groups back towards consensus, who smooths ruffled feathers and restores social harmony. This is emotional labour of the most subtle kind—invisible, absolutely essential to group function, and almost always unpaid in the currency of status, recognition, or professional advancement. She becomes the organisational nervous system whilst remaining unacknowledged as such.

Yet exceptions exist, and they are deeply instructive. The modern British woman on panels and in media is sharp, dry, and armed with irony as both sword and shield. She has learned to interrupt with precision and wit. She understands that humour can carry real authority, that a well-timed joke can demolish an argument more effectively than any direct contradiction. She recognises that the British conversational system, for all its apparent rigidity and opacity, has one crucial vulnerability: it is remarkably easy to dominate if you are willing to violate the unspoken rules with sufficient style and confidence. The woman who can interrupt, disagree fundamentally, and make everyone laugh whilst doing it has discovered a kind of backdoor into institutions that were explicitly designed to exclude her. It is not a perfect solution, and it still requires her to be clever in ways that men are not required to be, but it represents an evolution.

In France, political and intellectual discourse is an elegant battlefield where style counts as substance and form matters as much as content. Men still tend to speak more, and occupy more of the conversational space, but women who enter the arena often dominate through sheer linguistic precision and nuance. The Frenchwoman speaks with calibrated poise—measured, lyrical, slightly ironic. She does not shout; she insinuates. Her power lies in phrasing so exquisite that to interrupt her would feel like vandalism, like breaking something beautiful. Her sentences construct themselves as arguments; her digressions contain their own logic. She has learned that in a culture that worships eloquence, the most articulate voice wins, regardless of gender.

French feminism has historically tended towards the

philosophical rather than the activist, which means that discussions of gendered speech tend to sound like Foucauldian deconstructions of power relations rather than practical complaints about not getting a word in edgeways. This theoretical sophistication lends such discussions a certain authority within Parisian intellectual circles, but it also risks obscuring material realities beneath layers of linguistic beauty. Yet it is worth noting that this requirement for elegance, for refining anger into irony and passion into syntax, is itself a form of constraint—a rule that insists resistance be made beautiful before it can be acceptable.

In Southern Europe—Italy, Spain, and Greece—the situation is simultaneously more chaotic and more textured than in northern regions. The Mediterranean conversational style is inherently loud, interrupting, and simultaneously affectionate. Everyone talks at once, voices rising and falling like instruments in an orchestra without a conductor. Within this apparent chaos, gender dynamics are far more complex than simple dominance hierarchies would suggest. The Mediterranean man gestures expansively, declaims with passion, and occupies conversational space like a small but intense weather system —warm, overwhelming, utterly present. The Mediterranean woman counters with her own wit, her own rhythm, her own relentless persistence.

To the Northern European or American observer, it looks like conflict. To those raised within the system, it is actually a form of courtship, a dance of mutual respect and affection performed through loud disagreement. Conversation here is not a solo performance but a duet, and the woman who understands the music, who can match the rhythm and anticipate the tempo changes, can be every bit as dominant as any man. In fact, the stereotype of the Mediterranean matriarch—the woman who rules the home whilst allowing men their public prominence—suggests that gendered power in such societies may be distributed differently than in Anglo-Saxon or Northern

European contexts. The woman may not dominate the visible conversation, but she often dominates what matters.

Scandinavia presents an entirely different model. In Sweden, Norway, and Denmark, the egalitarian ethos has filtered down to conversational practice in ways that are genuinely instructive. Meetings are calm, orderly, and surprisingly inclusive. People wait for others to finish. Interruption is rare and, when it occurs, treated as a minor social transgression. The level playing field extends, in theory, to gender. A woman in a Scandinavian boardroom does not have to perform femininity or adopt masculine speech patterns. She can simply speak, and be heard as competent or incompetent based on what she actually says rather than how she says it or what her gender might suggest about her competence.

In practice, of course, no society has entirely transcended gender. But Scandinavia has come closer than most to creating conversational conditions where gender is less determinative of who gets heard. Whether this is because the societies themselves are more genuinely egalitarian or because they have simply become better at disguising remaining hierarchies is a question worth contemplating. The point is that it is possible. The Nordic model demonstrates that conversation can be restructured to be more equitable, that the problem is not innate to human nature but to the conversational systems we have constructed.

Eastern Europe occupies its own space. In Poland, Hungary, and the Balkans, the weight of history has produced interesting inversions. Publicly, in formal discourse and politics, men still dominate. Yet in private conversation, in families, in informal settings, the matriarch often rules with an authority both ancient and unquestioned. The Eastern European woman has historically been responsible for survival—literal, economic, emotional. She has seen empires rise and fall, ideologies proclaimed and abandoned. She speaks with the authority of someone who has managed complexity whilst men made speeches. The young women of Warsaw and Budapest are now reclaiming this authority for public spaces, speaking with the brisk, unsentimental directness of their grandmothers, allergic to flattery, assuming they will be heard. They have learned that femininity can be performed when convenient and abandoned when inconvenient, that the most effective conversational strategy is often to simply stop performing and start insisting.

The Middle East presents a case where gendered speech remains highly structured, yet contains within it complex negotiations and subtle forms of power. In many Arab societies, public discourse remains predominantly male. The spaces where formal authority is exercised, where political and religious power resides, are still coded masculine. Yet this is only the visible layer. Within families, within private gatherings, the female voice often carries authority equal to or exceeding that of men. The grandmother's wisdom, the mother's counsel—these remain central to decision-making in ways that Western observers sometimes fail to recognise because they are not exercised through formal speech but through conversation, narrative, and the transmission of values across generations.

Across Asia, the dynamics are equally complex and culturally specific. In Japan and Korea, younger women are beginning to push gently against linguistic deference, questioning why politeness must always mean invisibility. On television panels and in public spaces, women are claiming airtime with increasing confidence. Yet the underlying cultural value of harmony remains, which means that even progressive women tend to exercise influence through different mechanisms than direct confrontation or interruption. In India, where debate is quite literally a national sport, women have begun appearing on television panels with remarkable fearlessness, arguing politics, philosophy, and policy with directness that would have been unthinkable a generation ago. Yet across much of Asia, conversational dominance remains coded as masculine, and the voice that is deeper, louder, more insistent is still more likely to be perceived as authoritative.

The truth that emerges across all these cultural variations is that the "myth of balance" is precisely that—a myth. We speak of gender balance in conversation as though it is a neutral, technical problem that can be solved through training programmes and awareness campaigns. The reality is more fraught. What is required is not merely balance but a genuine reimagining of what conversation is for. If we believe conversation is primarily about information transfer, then gender might theoretically be irrelevant—may the best idea win. But conversation is not primarily about information transfer. It is about recognition, belonging, and the negotiation of power. And power, as every culture knows, has always flowed differently depending on gender.

Each culture has begun to grapple with this in its own way. The American solution has been to encourage women to be more aggressive, to "lean in," to adopt the conversational styles that have historically been rewarded. This has created a generation of women who can compete in traditionally male arenas, but it has not fundamentally changed the game—it has simply added more players to it. The British solution has been subtler: irony, wit, and the cultivation of exceptions. The French have theorised it into philosophical sophistication. The Scandinavians have attempted to flatten hierarchies altogether. The Eastern Europeans have drawn on historical memory of resilience. The Mediterranean cultures have acknowledged that power moves differently when you understand the music.

What is needed, perhaps, is not one solution but a genuine dialogue between these different approaches. The American insistence that women can speak loudly and be heard. The British understanding that style and wit can carry authority. The French commitment to elegance in language. The Scandinavian dedication to genuine inclusion. The Eastern

European knowledge that endurance is its own form of power. The Mediterranean appreciation for passion and rhythm. The Asian understanding that influence can flow through subtler channels. The African and Middle Eastern recognition that different forms of authority can coexist.

When women finally have the same freedom as men to speak loudly or softly, forcefully or gently, to interrupt or to listen, without those choices being interpreted through the lens of gender, then perhaps we will have achieved something worth calling balance. Until then, the loudness or quietness of women in any conversational space will always be a political statement, whether they intend it to be or not. The question is not whether women should be louder. The question is why we have made loudness the measure of being heard at all.

CHAPTER TEN: THE PUB PHILOSOPHER AND THE DINNER-TABLE DIPLOMAT

How the World Eats, Drinks, and Declares Its Opinions

Conversation changes the moment the cork is pulled. Alcohol and appetite loosen tongues, blur hierarchies, and transform social ritual into something more primal and honest. At the table, where sustenance is shared, the human voice finds its truest register. Across the world, every table has its own choreography of confidence: who speaks first, who listens longest, who refills the glass, who pretends to. The pub and the dinner table are humanity's oldest platforms for debate, philosophy, and the declaration of half-baked certainty served with conviction.

There is something about food that makes people speak more truthfully, or at least more boldly. The table is where hierarchy softens. You cannot maintain absolute authority whilst holding a fork. The mouth occupied with sustenance becomes a mouth less capable of dominance. Somewhere between the starter and the main course, something shifts. Ties are loosened, guards are dropped, and the second glass of wine arrives with permission implicit. By dessert, philosophy has been attempted, certainties have been proclaimed, and the world has been fixed, at least temporarily, by people who barely understand it. By coffee, nobody quite remembers what was decided, but everyone leaves believing their point was made.

The British pub remains the most perfect laboratory for studying national character expressed through conversation. The pub is democracy with a head of foam. In theory, everyone is equal once the first pint hits the table, which is precisely why it instantly fills with amateur economists, football managers, and foreign-policy experts, all absolutely convinced of their expertise. The Pub Philosopher begins quietly, almost sheepishly, as though apologising for having a thought at all. "The thing about inflation, right..." Within minutes, he has quoted Churchill, misquoted Keynes, and explained in granular detail how he personally would fix the NHS if only someone would listen. His audience nods, half-listening, already formulating their own turn, their own chance to make the same point with slightly more authority.

By closing time, no problem remains unsolved and no listener unconquered. It is British conversation distilled to its essence: witty, circular, heroically certain until the morning arrives and the world has not, in fact, changed one iota based on three hours of pub philosophy. Yet there is something rather touching about it—the faith that talking things through will produce understanding, even as decades of experience suggest otherwise. The British pub philosopher is not malicious. He is simply a believer in the power of talk. He thinks words matter. He thinks listening happens. He thinks his point will resonate. By morning, he has usually forgotten what his point was, but the faith remains eternal.

In France, the dinner invitation is an intellectual ambush disguised as hospitality. You arrive expecting a pleasant evening. You leave having survived a philosophical interrogation of your entire worldview. The food is exquisite—that goes without saying—but the debate is inevitable and often exhausting. Around the table, wine lubricates philosophy with dangerous efficiency. The host opens with a question seemingly innocent but carefully chosen to provoke: "Mais qu'est-ce que la liberté aujourd'hui?" What is freedom today? And suddenly, dessert is delayed by an hour, the cheese course abandoned, everyone mid-argument about something that began as a simple question and has expanded into a full deconstruction of Western philosophy.

Interruptions fly like rapiers across the table. Guests quote Rousseau with the casualness of other people quoting football scores. They argue semiotics over the fish course. They invoke Foucault whilst discussing the wine. It is not arrogance; it is civic duty. To dine without debate would be barbarism, a failure of hospitality, an insult to the food and the company. The French dinner table is a parliament in miniature, and everyone present understands that their job is to contribute fully to the intellectual commons. By the end, no consensus has been reached, but everyone has had the pleasure of their own thoughts refined through contradiction. That is the point. Not agreement, but engagement.

An Italian dinner is not discussion in any conventional sense; it is aria. Multiple voices overlap in magnificent disregard for turn-taking. Hands conduct invisible orchestras. Emotion trumps evidence every time. Everyone interrupts because the entire culture understands that interruption means passion, that to speak over someone is to show you care enough to engage. The meal follows its own dramatic arc—the antipasti as prelude, the primi as rising action, the secondi as climax, the dolci as collective reconciliation. Arguments that seemed irreconcilable over the main course dissolve into laughter and hugs by the time coffee arrives. Family remains intact. Politics are forgiven. The conversation, no matter how heated, is always ultimately about belonging.

Spanish dinner conversation has its own rhythm, its own particular warmth. The meal is never truly finished; it simply transitions. Tapas ensure there is never a full stop, never a moment when conversation must conclude because the food has run out. You eat, you talk, you move, you keep talking. Debate here is rhythmic, building in waves of laughter, storytelling, spontaneous applause. No one owns the floor; it passes like a plate being shared. The Spanish secret, if there is one, is this: disagreement without disconnection. Voices rise, hands fly through the air, points are made forcefully, but affection remains constant. The skill is to argue fiercely and forgive immediately, to disagree about everything whilst genuinely liking everyone.

In Germany and Central Europe, dining takes on a more structured quality. In Berlin or Vienna, dinner is less improvisation and more symposium. Arguments are logical, sequenced, politely ferocious. One person speaks, others listen, then they counter with equal rigour. In Prague, the conversation grows darker and drier with each beer: history intrudes, tragedy whispers in the background, absurdity becomes the default lens. By the third round, laughter has replaced hope—a victory of irony over despair. The Eastern European dinner table is therapy by debate, confession through argument. The national toast becomes stand-in for the therapist's couch: "To surviving ourselves." It is not warm in the way Mediterranean dinners are warm, but it is honest. At an Eastern European table, you will not be flattered, but you will be understood.

Scandinavia operates according to entirely different principles. In Sweden or Norway, silence at dinner is not failure; it is flavour. The meal proceeds with a kind of peaceful contemplation. People speak when they have something genuinely worth saying, which turns out to be rarely. But when they do speak, it lands with the weight of truth. The wine flows slowly, the conversation slower. Any disagreement is gentle, phrased as a question: "Could it be otherwise?" By dessert, consensus has somehow been achieved without anyone noticing it was being negotiated. Everyone leaves satisfied, not because they have won, but because they have been heard fairly. The meal has been about nourishment in every sense.

From Belgrade to Sarajevo, the Balkan table is theatre. The

patriarch begins with a story, the matriarch corrects it halfway through, cousins join in from various angles, and the night becomes a living novel written in real time. Each toast grows longer, more philosophical, more patriotic, until someone inevitably sings. It is chaos—beautiful, cultural, thoroughly alive. Here, talk is survival. Laughter is defiance. No one wins the argument because the point was never victory; it was belonging. The table is not meant to produce decisions; it is meant to produce togetherness. In a region where history has been violent and unpredictable, the dinner table becomes a space where people know everyone will still be there when the evening ends.

In the Arab world, conversation flows around the table like coffee—strong, sweet, continuous, and never-ending. The rhythm of hospitality sets the tempo of discourse. You talk to honour the host. You listen to honour the guest. You speak, but always with awareness of the social architecture holding everyone up. The Dinner-Table Diplomat is born here, out of necessity and culture merged into something graceful. He disagrees without disrespect. He praises before critiquing. He corrects errors with a proverb, embedding truth within poetry. Every argument ends not in victory but in generosity: "Eat, my friend—we can discuss this again tomorrow." It is empathy with structure, pride softened by poetry, conviction expressed through courtesy.

Across East and Southeast Asia, meals mirror order. In Japan or Korea, elders speak first and juniors wait their turn. Debate is subtle, framed by ritual and restraint. The hierarchy is invisible but absolute. Harmony matters more than victory because the group matters more than any individual within it. In China, conversation at dinner is strategic. Deals are made between courses. Truths are spoken in metaphor. You must listen to what is not being said, must understand the subtext beneath the surface. In India, the dinner table is carnival and chaos: religion, cricket, corruption, philosophy, all happening simultaneously, yet somehow in rhythm. Everyone talks at once, but with an underlying structure that only insiders truly understand.

The North African and Middle Eastern majlis tradition transfers seamlessly to the dinner table. The conversation is communal, fluid, performative in the best sense. It is not about dominance but about generating communal energy. The meal becomes an extension of the majlis—people gathered to share food, story, and time. Speaking is participation in something larger than individual ego. The table becomes a parliament where everyone has voice and everyone has duty to contribute to collective meaning.

Why does the table matter so profoundly? Because it is where hierarchy softens, where masks come loose, where the world is remade through conversation. The pub philosopher and the dinner-table diplomat represent two poles of humanity: one convinced he is right, absolutely certain of his own wisdom; the other hoping everyone stays friends whilst truth is negotiated gently. Every culture oscillates between them—certainty and civility, declaration and diplomacy, the insistence that one's point matters and the recognition that everyone else's does too.

The universal toast exists in every nation, yet it is never universal. The British clink glasses awkwardly, unsure where to look. The French say santé with elegant brevity. The Poles declare na zdrowie with conviction that borders on aggression. The Italians shout cin-cin! like an encore, requiring repetition, requiring that everyone participate. The Japanese bow slightly over kanpai, the gesture itself a form of speech. The Arabs raise tiny cups of coffee and say sahtein—"two healths." The Germans toast with Prost! The Spanish with salud! Different words across languages, same underlying wish: may we survive one another's opinions. May this meal, and this conversation, not end in disaster. May we leave this table still friends, or at least still speaking.

The food serves a function beyond nourishment. It is the excuse, the vehicle, the third participant in conversation. Discuss the meal, and you avoid discussing anything truly dangerous. Praise the wine, and you have made a statement about the host's taste. Eat slowly, and you signal you are comfortable, unhurried, ready to stay for hours. Eat quickly, and you suggest either hunger or anxiety to escape. The whole repertoire of human emotion is expressed through how we behave around the table.

Modern life has threatened this ancient ritual. The business lunch has become something faster, more transactional. The family dinner has been fragmented into individual meals consumed whilst looking at screens. The pub has been replaced by the networking event, where people speak at each other rather than with each other. Yet whenever humans gather around food, something ancient reasserts itself. The pace slows. The voices deepen. The conversation becomes real.

At the best tables, across all cultures, something remarkable happens: people become temporarily equal. The CEO and the student, the famous and the forgotten, the young and the old —all equally hungry, all equally dependent on what is shared. In this moment of equality, real conversation becomes possible. Not the performance we give online or in boardrooms, but the actual exchange of ideas, worries, dreams, and doubts.

The table is where civilisation happens. Not in parliaments or universities, but in kitchens and dining rooms, pubs and cafés, majlis and family compounds. It is where understanding is built, brick by brick, meal by meal, conversation by conversation. It is where the pub philosopher learns he does not know everything, and where the dinner-table diplomat learns that diplomacy alone cannot solve everything. It is where we remember that we are animals first, philosophical second, and that both are necessary.

Conclusion: Talk, Eat, Repeat

The table will always reveal what the screen conceals. In digital life, we broadcast; at the table, we belong. No algorithm yet replicates the chemistry of shared bread and shared contradiction. The performance ends when the food arrives. We are reduced to our humanity—hungry, social, in need of being heard and needing to hear others. And if sometimes the pub philosopher shouts too loud, or the dinner-table diplomat smooths too much, so be it. Better noise over food than silence online. Because every great civilisation—from Athens to Aleppo, from Kraków to Kyoto—began not with a declaration or a decree, but with a meal. And in that meal, the real conversation about how to live together began.

CHAPTER ELEVEN: THE SILENCE EXTINCTION

Why Pauses Terrify the Modern World

Silence used to be the punctuation of civilisation. A comma was rest. A full stop was reflection. The space between words was where thought lived, where meaning could settle and be properly understood. Now silence is treated like a glitch in the system, a failure of connection, a moment of profound awkwardness that must be rectified immediately with noise, any noise, something to prove that the line is still active and the person is still there. We rush to fill every gap—with words, notifications, music, the ambient hum of perpetual connectivity. But silence, that ancient currency of thought, has become almost unspendable in modern conversation.

We have forgotten what silence is for. It is not emptiness. It is not failure. It is the space where understanding grows, where complexity can be contemplated, where the next sentence can be constructed with care rather than panic. Every culture once used silence differently, and those differences reveal something profound about what each society values. In the desert, silence meant reverence. In the monastery, it meant reflection. In diplomacy, it meant strategy. In love, it meant trust. Today, it means someone has lost their Wi-Fi connection, and every visible person is checking their phone to see if you are still there.

We have come to measure engagement by decibels rather than

depth. The pause, once a mark of wisdom and consideration, now signals weakness or uncertainty. The quiet person is not mysterious but "off the grid." The modern world talks over its own echo, creating a feedback loop of noise that drowns out any possibility of actual reflection. We are so afraid of silence that we have filled the world with sound, and in doing so, we have made it impossible to hear anything clearly.

In Scandinavia, silence remains an active verb rather than a passive state. In Sweden, Finland, and Norway, silence is still understood as a form of communication. A conversation without deliberate gaps is considered aggressive; a person who fills every pause is viewed with suspicion, as though they cannot be trusted to think before they speak. The Nordic pause is intentional—space carved out for thought, for honesty, for breath itself. It says: I am listening so carefully that I need time to respond appropriately. In Nordic boardrooms, meetings proceed with what foreigners find deeply unsettling: long stretches where nobody speaks. Everyone simply sits, thinking. Then, after a small eternity has passed, someone says, "Yes," and it carries the weight of complete agreement or complete understanding. It means everything that needed to be said has been comprehended.

To the Nordic ear, silence is not absence—it is presence. It is respect made audible through its opposite. It is the understanding that meaning lives not just in words but in the space between them. This is why business meetings in Stockholm or Oslo feel unnerving to Americans or Brazilians accustomed to constant verbal affirmation. The Nordic silence is not comfortable in the way continuous chatter is comfortable; it is satisfying in the way a completed thought is satisfying. It requires patience. It requires trust. It requires the belief that the other person is thinking as carefully as you are.

Japan has an entire philosophy of silence embedded in its language and culture. There is a word for it: ma—the meaningful interval between things. It is not simply the space; it is the space as content. A pause in Japanese conversation is not empty; it is charged with awareness and presence. The Japanese listener's response—an aizuchi, a small sound or nod—signals presence without interruption. It says: I am here, I am listening, I am tracking your thought, please continue. For Westerners accustomed to conversational clutter, to the constant need to fill air with affirmation and response, this stillness feels deeply uncomfortable, like being left on read by someone standing directly in front of you. But within that calm is extraordinary sensitivity—the understanding that meaning lives as much in the spaces as in the sound. The West speaks to fill time; Japan listens to inhabit it.

In Eastern Europe, silence carries a different quality altogether. It is not meditative; it is wary. It is the residue of times when words could wound or condemn, when carelessly spoken thoughts could trigger consequences. Older generations learned that discretion could save careers, families, lives. Even today, silence in Eastern Europe carries moral gravity. You speak when it matters; otherwise, you think. The pause is not comfortable but courageous—the moment before truth is spoken, the moment after it has landed. Westerners sometimes misread this as coldness or disengagement. It is not. It is a learned economy of speech, empathy expressed through endurance rather than echo. When an Eastern European friend sits with you in quiet solidarity, they are not avoiding you. They are honouring the moment. They are saying: this matters too much for careless words.

France maintains a complicated relationship with silence. In formal debate and intellectual discourse, silence is deliberately curated. The well-timed pause is theatre—a way to make words taste richer when they return, like the silence between movements in a symphony. It is the space where the audience leans in. But dinner-table silence is another matter entirely: an unforgivable social sin. A lull in conversation during a meal means the wine is poor or the host uninspired. Someone will rescue it immediately with a quotation from Voltaire or a digression into philosophy. For the French, silence in public company is power; silence in company is catastrophe. You can be silent and mysterious. You cannot be silent and rude.

In Italy and Spain, silence signals only one thing: something is profoundly wrong. A quiet Italian is either ill or plotting revenge. A silent Spaniard has emotionally left the room. Here, talk is oxygen. To refuse it is to withdraw from life itself. Noise means connection; quiet feels like neglect. Where Northern Europe worships stillness as a form of wisdom, the South worships sound as a form of love. The ability to sit in silence would feel, to a Mediterranean person, like sitting in emotional darkness. Yet even here, silence appears—fleeting, dramatic, and sacred. At the end of a passionate argument, after an eruption of laughter, before the next espresso arrives—a pause emerges, shared, glowing with humanity. It lasts three seconds, maybe four, before someone interrupts it with "Anyway..." But for those brief seconds, it feels divine.

In the Arab world, silence retains its sacred dimension in ways that much of the modern world has abandoned. It lives in the rhythm of prayer, in the respectful interval before response, in the solemnity of a majlis when elders speak. To interrupt such quiet is to break honour. The Dinner-Table Diplomat, discussed in our previous chapter, knows this instinctively: a pause allows dignity to breathe. It signals respect for what has just been said. It creates space for the other person's words to settle before new ones arrive. Silence here is not empty; it is full of recognition. It is the conversational equivalent of bowing.

Across much of East and Southeast Asia, the pause is understood as wisdom embodied. In India, silence lives in conversation as the space before advice is given, the moment of reflection that proves you have listened. In China, it signifies consideration —the stillness before strategy, the moment where response is being calibrated to maximum effectiveness. In Korea, silence shows respect: thoughtfulness as social currency. The Asian pause is discipline—language's inhale before the exhale of response. It is how complexity becomes clarity. It is how someone demonstrates that they take your words seriously enough to think before replying.

Across Africa, conversation flows like music—speech followed by response, followed by silence, followed by the rhythm of communal understanding. The pause is pulse. It allows laughter to land, lets proverbs resonate, gives stories room to breathe. In the storytelling circles of Ghana or Kenya, silence means anticipation, not discomfort. The listener's hush is half the performance. The pause here is communal—meaning made in rhythm, not volume. The story and the silence are partners, each giving the other meaning.

In the Americas, the relationship with silence is far more fraught. In the United States, silence is seen as failure. A pause in conversation registers as awkwardness or, worse, as disagreement. Every pause must be filled—with data, reassurance, enthusiasm, a joke, anything to restore the flow. The American impulse is generous but exhausting: constant warmth mistaken for connection. In Latin America, silence is suspense, the intake of breath before the next burst of warmth or music. The continent of motion pauses only for spectacle, never for reflection. Both North and South America treat silence as something to escape rather than something to inhabit.

Why do we fear silence so profoundly? Because it exposes us. Without noise, there is no mask—just thought, raw and unfiltered. The pause confronts us with the possibility that we might not have something worth saying. It invites self-examination. It creates space for doubt. But that is precisely where meaning begins—not in the noise we make, but in the space we leave for others. The pause is where we acknowledge that we do not have all the answers. It is humility made audible through its opposite.

The modern world has declared total war on silence. Technology conspires against it at every turn. Notifications buzz. Algorithms whisper. Podcasts fill the commute. Background music accompanies every moment. Even in solitude, we stream content over silence. We have trained ourselves to fear the moment when the noise ends and our own thoughts start speaking back. We have created a civilisation where distraction is not a vice but a virtue, where the inability to sit quietly for five minutes is not a problem but a sign of engagement with the world.

Yet silence persists. It survives in churches, forests, libraries, and occasionally in conversation between people who trust each other enough not to fill the air. It exists in the moment before someone speaks an important truth. It lives in the space after someone has been truly heard. And it remains, despite everything, one of the most powerful tools of communication ever invented.

The psychology beneath our fear of silence is worth examining. Silence is vulnerability. It is the admission that we are not constantly producing, constantly performing, constantly proving our existence through noise. It is the radical act of being without broadcasting being. In a culture addicted to amplification, to constant self-promotion, to the documentation of every moment, silence feels like erasure. If you are not online, you are not alive—or so the logic of modern existence insists. But this is precisely the lie that silence reveals. We are alive in the quiet moments too. Perhaps more alive, because we are actually present.

Each culture offers a remedy to the silence extinction. From Scandinavia: disconnect regularly, and trust the silence to restore you. From Japan: respect ma, the space between things—it contains meaning. From Eastern Europe: let silence carry solidarity, not judgment. From the Middle East: use pauses to confer dignity on the speaker. From Africa: feel the rhythm between words; silence is part of the music. From Britain: turn awkwardness into artistry; the pause can be powerful. From France: control the silence strategically; it can amplify what comes after. From the Mediterranean: let emotion rest before it rises again; the pause allows the heart to catch up with the voice. From the Americas: rediscover quiet without guilt; stillness is not failure.

The next great revolution in communication may not be a new platform or a more efficient technology. It may be something far simpler and far more radical: the deliberate pause. The conscious choice to stop speaking and listen. The refusal to fill every gap with content. The courage to sit with ambiguity, to tolerate the discomfort of not knowing what to say next, to trust that meaning can emerge from silence as surely as from speech.

Silence is not the opposite of conversation. It is its essential component. Every great speaker understands this. Every wise person knows it. The most eloquent silence is the one that follows truth, or precedes it. The most powerful moment in any dialogue is often the one where no one is speaking—when everyone is processing, thinking, allowing the words to settle.

Conclusion: The Quiet Renaissance

Perhaps silence is not extinct—merely endangered. It survives in the margins, in the spaces between screens, in the moments before the next notification arrives. It persists in cultures that have not yet fully surrendered to the noise economy. It waits in forests and libraries and quiet rooms where people still believe that thinking matters more than broadcasting thought.

The rediscovery of silence may be the most important conversational skill of the coming decades. Not the silence of avoidance or awkwardness, but the silence of presence. The silence that says: I am listening so carefully that I need time to respond. The silence that creates space for others to think.

The silence that acknowledges complexity too deep for quick answers.

Because after all the words, after all the arguments and broadcasts and performances, the most eloquent line in any conversation might still be the one no one utters. The pause where understanding happens. The silence where meaning lives. The space where, if we are very quiet, very still, and very brave, we might actually hear one another.

CHAPTER TWELVE: THE AGGRESSIVE AGREEER

How Consensus Became a Contact Sport

Few conversational creatures are as cunningly disguised as the Aggressive Agreeer. They never contradict, never challenge, never raise their voice in anger. Yet somehow, despite this apparent civility, they manage to dominate every exchange with remarkable efficiency. They smile, nod, and echo your words with the intensity of a hostage video: "Exactly! Totally agree! That's so true!" And then, in the next breath—so smoothly you almost miss the pivot—they expand, reinterpret, and replace your point until it becomes unrecognisable. Agreement, in their hands, is not kindness or support. It is conquest dressed in warmth. It is dominance with a smile.

The Aggressive Agreeer is a product of modern corporate culture and therapy-speak merged into something more insidious: the weaponisation of positivity. They represent an evolution in conversational predation. Where the old dominators shouted, the new ones nod. Where previous generations bullied, the Aggressive Agreeer hugs you to death with validation. They are the conversational equivalent of a python: they agree so completely that you do not notice you are being squeezed until it is too late.

The evolution of this species is worth tracing. Once upon a time, open disagreement was considered healthy, even necessary.

People debated, clashed, occasionally learned something. Conflict was uncomfortable but productive. Then came the age of diplomacy, diversity training, and HR-approved civility. Disagreement became dangerous—impolite, unprofessional, potentially "toxic." The word "toxic" itself became a kind of conversational nuclear weapon, deployed to silence any form of genuine dissent. And into this vacuum stepped the Aggressive Agreeer: the modern world's smiling assassin of nuance, the master of the soft coup.

They do not fight you. They absorb you. They do not contradict; they "build on your point." They do not dismiss; they "totally get where you're coming from, and here's what I think we should do instead." Which is to say, they dismiss completely whilst performing understanding. It is perhaps the most insidious form of conversational dominance precisely because it masquerades as connection.

Nowhere thrives this species like the United States. The American version of the Aggressive Agreeer is raised on motivational slogans and customer-service smiles, perfecting agreement as a cultural instinct. In the corporate world, in schools, in families, the American Agreeer has learned that every idea is "great," every opinion is "interesting," and every person is "awesome." This is not cynicism—not entirely—but rather a kind of enforced positivity that makes genuine disagreement feel like personal rejection. The Aggressive Agreeer begins with validation: "I love where you're going with this. What if we completely changed it?" The victim nods along, hypnotised by the initial affirmation, only to realise midway through the second sentence that their entire premise has been dismantled.

In the American corporate ecosystem, the Aggressive Agreeer is king. They have mastered the art of confrontation without consequence. They begin by saying, "I totally agree with you," which immediately puts the listener in a defensive position—if you disagree with what they say next, you are disagreeing with yourself. It is conversational judo, using the opponent's own momentum against them. The result is pure American genius: disagreement without visible conflict, dominance without accountability. The meeting ends with everyone nodding, and nobody quite remembers how the original proposal became its opposite.

Britain's Aggressive Agreeer operates with even greater subtlety. Here, overt confrontation is considered vulgar. So instead, the British version cloaks their power play in layers of deference and charm. "Quite right," they say—then proceed to quietly dismantle you with data, with anecdotes, with perfectly deployed irony. In meetings, they are deadly. They agree so elaborately that by the time they have finished, no one remembers what was being discussed. The original speaker nods along, hypnotised by civility, only to realise too late that they have been politely erased.

This is the empire of understatement at work. The British Aggressive Agreeer does not shout you down; they make you disappear through a fog of agreeable language. They agree with your premise whilst destroying your conclusion. They validate your feelings whilst invalidating your argument. And they do it all with such charm that you leave feeling somehow grateful for having been bested. It is psychological mastery dressed as politeness.

France takes aggressive agreement into more philosophical territory. The French rarely shout, "Yes!" in the way Americans do. Instead, they say, "Je suis d'accord, mais..." ("I agree, but...")—and that "but" is an art form in itself. It introduces a miniature essay, complete with historical footnotes and quotations from dead philosophers. The French Aggressive Agreeer does not hijack your thought; they refine it into something distinctly their own—polished, provocative, and ever so slightly superior. It is the conversational equivalent of a museum restoration:

your idea remains visible beneath the varnish of theirs, but you are no longer certain it is the same painting.

In Eastern Europe, aggressive agreement takes on an entirely different flavour, one tinged with irony and weariness. Here, agreement is rarely straightforward. "Yes, of course," can mean "No, obviously not," and everyone in the room understands this perfectly. This is the land of the sceptical yes—a tiny nod loaded with centuries of experience in saying the socially correct thing whilst meaning something entirely different. The Eastern European Aggressive Agreeer does not gush or perform enthusiasm. They smirk. They allow you your fantasy before gently puncturing it with reality.

"Sure, that will definitely work," they say, in a tone of voice that communicates: I have survived worse than this foolish idea, and I will survive this too. Their weapon is irony—the elegant refusal to be fooled twice by the same mechanism. Where Americans use enthusiasm as camouflage, Eastern Europeans use cynicism. Where the British deploy charm, Eastern Europeans deploy weary understanding. It is aggressive agreement performed by people too intelligent to pretend it is anything other than what it is: a polite form of "No."

Scandinavia produces a different species altogether: the Passive Consensus Builder. They do not seem aggressive at all. They nod slowly, say, "Interesting point," and then produce a better one—delivered with no trace of ego, leaving you grateful for your own defeat. In these egalitarian cultures, open dominance is frowned upon. So power expresses itself through consensus. Everyone "agrees"—and somehow, the most persuasive voice always happens to set the final version of the minutes. Agreement, here, is government policy. It is dominance through democracy, victory through consensus.

The Nordic Aggressive Agreeer is perhaps the most effective version precisely because they appear not to be aggressive at all. They listen, they pause, they synthesise. By the time they have finished presenting "their thoughts," it turns out they were everyone's thoughts all along. You have been led to a predetermined conclusion so gently that you believe you arrived there yourself. It is Machiavelli in minimalist clothing.

In Italy, Spain, and Greece, people rarely agree quietly. When they say "Yes!", it comes with exclamation marks, gesture, and emotional endorsement. But listen closely: their "yes" is often followed by five minutes of contradiction. It is not hypocrisy —it is rhythm. The Mediterranean Aggressive Agreeer does not seek control; they seek connection. They echo you loudly so you know you have been heard, even if they have not actually listened. It is performance masquerading as empathy.

The Middle East approaches aggressive agreement as an art form, one where diplomacy and politeness form the foundation. Across the Arab world, agreement is etiquette. Harmony maintains honour. To contradict directly would risk embarrassment—a breach of the unspoken social contract of respect. So the Aggressive Agreeer thrives in politeness. "Yes, my friend, of course," they say warmly, with genuine affection —and then steer the discussion toward their desired outcome with such elegance and hospitality that you lose the argument without noticing. It is persuasion through generosity: you lose the debate but leave full, flattered, and oddly grateful.

Across East and Southeast Asia, the "yes" often hides entire paragraphs of "no." To disagree publicly is to break face; to agree is to preserve harmony. In Japan, the phrase "Yes, I understand" (hai, wakarimashita) does not mean agreement. It means: I have heard you, and we will quietly do something else. In China, consensus is strategic—the first step in negotiation, not its conclusion. In India, where talk flows like monsoon rain, everyone agrees enthusiastically until it is time to act. Then half vanish and the rest reinterpret the agreement entirely.

These are cultures that understand the value of verbal illusion —agreement as choreography rather than capitulation. The

Aggressive Agreeer here does not waste energy on Western-style dominance. They work through subtler channels: hierarchies, face, and the understanding that what is said in public and what is done in private operate according to different rules entirely.

Across much of Africa, open disagreement is seen as impolite. Meetings and councils aim for unity; dissent is folded into narrative rather than shouted from the rooftops. The Aggressive Agreeer here may nod along, but their silence carries judgement. They will agree in public and correct in private—a form of social intelligence that preserves community over ego. Agreement, in this sense, is strategic kindness, a way of maintaining relationships whilst still registering disagreement through channels that do not rupture the social fabric.

The global business of "yes" reveals itself most clearly in international meetings. These are Babel rendered in PowerPoint, where every participant speaks a different dialect of agreement. The American says, "Absolutely!" meaning, "We will think about it." The Brit says, "Right, yes," meaning, "Let us never speak of this again." The German says, "I agree in principle," meaning, "You are approximately 60 percent wrong." The Indian says, "Yes, yes," meaning, "We shall see." The Chinese delegate nods, meaning, "No, but thank you for your enthusiasm."

It is a Tower of Babel constructed entirely out of agreement, a global symphony of people saying yes whilst meaning anything but. The minutes will record that consensus was reached. The reality is that nothing has been agreed upon; everyone has simply performed agreement well enough that the meeting could end. Aggressive agreement, deployed at scale across cultures, becomes a system for avoiding actual decision-making. It is the modern corporation's greatest achievement: the ability to have meetings without resolving anything.

Why do we agree aggressively rather than disagree honestly? Because disagreement exposes us. It creates conflict, invites retaliation, risks rejection or professional consequences. So we hide behind consensus, hoping politeness will substitute for progress. We have learned that the path of least resistance is agreement, even when it is false. But fake agreement corrodes trust faster than honest dissent. When everyone nods, nothing moves. When the room is full of yes-sayers, the actual problems get worse.

The psychology of the Aggressive Agreeer is worth understanding. Their behaviour is not entirely cynical. They crave connection, harmony, approval. Their weaponised warmth is self-defence—an attempt to control uncertainty through constant affirmation. They live by an unspoken rule: if everyone is smiling, nothing can hurt me. But beneath that glow of validation lies exhaustion—the emotional burnout of people who have mistaken likability for love, who believe that if they are kind enough to everyone, everyone will be kind to them. The tragedy is that aggressive agreement often achieves the opposite: it creates distance precisely because it prevents genuine connection.

Every society offers its own antidote to this disease of false positivity. From America: keep the enthusiasm, but lose the flattery. Actually disagree sometimes. Actually say no. From Britain: keep the politeness, but add honesty. Your irony is elegant, but it also obscures. Say what you mean occasionally. From Eastern Europe: retain the irony, but share the optimism. Not everything is doomed. From Asia: preserve harmony, but invite authenticity. You can maintain relationships whilst disagreeing. From the Mediterranean: keep the warmth, but shorten the speech. Your passion is beautiful, but it can also overwhelm. From the Nordics: keep the silence, but allow disagreement. Consensus should not mean conformity.

The cure for toxic agreement is courage. Courage to say, "I do not agree," without softening it with apology. Courage to let disagreement exist without it destroying the relationship. Courage to believe that real connection is built on honesty, not on constant affirmation. This is not easy in cultures that have been trained to smooth over conflict, to prioritise harmony over truth. But it is necessary.

Conclusion: The Courage of No

In an age that confuses kindness with conformity, the word "no" has become revolutionary. It does not have to be cruel, abrupt, or final. It can be the most respectful sound in the world—the sound of someone actually listening, actually thinking, actually taking the conversation seriously enough to disagree.

Because when everyone says "yes," conversation dies. The room becomes a echo chamber of false consensus where nothing real is discussed and nothing real is decided. But when someone dares to say "no"—genuinely, thoughtfully, respectfully—thinking begins. The conversation becomes real. The stakes become apparent. And suddenly, the possibility of actual understanding emerges from beneath the rubble of false agreement.

The Aggressive Agreeer believes they are protecting themselves and others through constant positivity. In truth, they are preventing growth. Real conversation requires the courage to disagree, the willingness to be changed, and the strength to say no when no is what needs to be said. Everything else is just pleasant noise.

CHAPTER THIRTEEN: THE FEEDBACK LOOP OF DOOM

When Every Voice Starts Sounding Like Ours

We built the internet to connect humanity. We ended up connecting ourselves—to ourselves. What began as the greatest conversation in human history has become the loudest monologue ever recorded. Billions of people, one enormous mirror. Every click takes us deeper into reflection of our own beliefs. Every algorithm learns what we already think and shows us more of it. We have constructed the most perfect echo chamber ever imagined, and we inhabit it willingly, even gratefully, mistaking the sound of our own voice for dialogue.

Welcome to the Feedback Loop of Doom: a system so perfectly engineered to keep us trapped in our own certainty that escape has become nearly impossible. The platforms promised connection. They delivered isolation wrapped in the illusion of community. They promised amplification of our voice. They delivered amplification of our biases. They promised that we would find our people. We did—millions of them, all thinking exactly like us, all confirming what we already believe, all providing validation that what we think is correct and everyone who disagrees is not just wrong but evil, stupid, or both.

The modern algorithm is the ultimate Aggressive Agreeer. It never argues, never doubts, never says, "Perhaps you are mistaken." It just nods and feeds you more of what you already believe. Every click tightens the loop. You engage with outrage, and the algorithm rewards you with more outrage. You click on validation, and validation multiplies. You watch a video confirming your political beliefs, and suddenly your entire feed is people who think exactly as you do, all equally certain, all equally wrong about different things, yet all equally convinced of their rightness.

The system is not ideological; it is biochemical. The algorithm does not care what you believe—it cares that you believe it strongly enough to keep engaging. Outrage and validation both produce dopamine. Fear and affirmation both keep you scrolling. The machine is indifferent to truth; it cares only about engagement. And engagement, it turns out, is easier to generate through certainty than through nuance. A complicated, ambiguous statement will not hold your attention. A provocative, absolute declaration will.

We are not addicted to information—we are addicted to confirmation. The algorithm exploits a weakness as old as human nature: we prefer to be right more than we prefer to be accurate. We would rather encounter people who agree with us than people who might teach us something. We would rather win an argument than understand an opponent. The feedback loop simply industrialised this tendency, made it systematic, and scaled it to billions.

In the United States, debate has become a spectator sport with corporate sponsors. Cable news, podcasts, and TikTok rants all sell the same product: righteous certainty delivered with studio lighting and a soundtrack. The American feed runs on emotional calories—fear, pride, empathy, outrage—all served supersized with extra helpings of hysteria. You do not scroll for facts; you scroll for team spirit. Even disagreement has been rebranded as engagement. A million angry comments are a marketing strategy. The algorithm celebrates conflict because conflict keeps people clicking.

The feedback loop here is patriotic: "Your opinion matters... as long as it is loud." The American internet rewards those who are most certain, most vocal, most willing to express absolute conviction about complex problems. Nuance is punished with invisibility. Ambiguity is treated as weakness. The result is a nation that has become increasingly polarised not because Americans have fundamentally different values, but because the platforms are designed to make them seem that way.

British social media thrives on irony and sarcasm. Nothing is said without a wink, a meme, or an apologetic ellipsis. The national pastime online is performative cynicism: complaining loudly whilst pretending not to care. "This country is a disaster... anyway, tea?" The algorithm adores this rhythm—the oscillation between outrage and dismissal keeps engagement perfectly calibrated to British sensibilities. It is the digital version of the pub argument: nobody wins, everyone feels slightly clever, and you leave believing you have accomplished something meaningful when in fact nothing has changed.

The British feedback loop is particularly insidious because irony allows people to express extremism whilst maintaining plausible deniability. You can post something genuinely harmful and claim you were "just joking" or "being ironic." The sarcasm becomes both shield and weapon. The algorithm, unable to detect irony, treats it as engagement and promotes it. Meanwhile, the boundary between actual belief and performed belief dissolves. By the time irony has been repeated enough times, it stops being irony and becomes actual conviction.

In Eastern Europe, the online conversation feels like a family argument that has lasted since 1945. Sarcasm is armour; irony, oxygen. The typical Polish or Czech commenter treats conspiracy theories the way others treat weather: notice, mock, move on. Yet cynicism can curdle into fatalism. If you have learned that systems rarely tell the truth, the algorithm's half-truths feel almost comforting. Better to be cynically correct than naively surprised. The Eastern European feedback loop feeds on resignation: nothing changes, so why not laugh? The algorithm learns this and serves up more reasons to be cynical.

There is something almost logical about the Eastern European response to the feedback loop. In a region where propaganda was state policy and official truth was consistently lies, the internet feels familiar. It is another system telling you what to believe. The difference is that now you can choose which lies comfort you. The feedback loop does not feel particularly sinister because it is just the continuation of a pattern people have lived with for generations: the understanding that what is said officially is never what is actually true.

France maintains its intellectual fury online. Twitter—if it can still be called that—in France is an endless salon where every disagreement becomes a manifesto. The algorithm rewards the most elegant indignation. Outrage must come dressed in theory. A scandal is not truly scandalous until someone references Foucault. Thus the feedback loop in France produces not noise but literature: la polémique as performance. The French are furious online, but they are furious with style. They disagree brilliantly, and the algorithm, recognising engagement, promotes their brilliance.

The French feedback loop has an intellectual veneer that makes it feel more legitimate than other versions. You are not just angry; you are philosophically correct. Your outrage is not emotional; it is rational, grounded in theory, supported by history. The algorithm learns this and serves up more intellectual arguments, more citations, more proof that your anger is justified. It is a feedback loop for the mind: thought reinforcing thought, certainty building on certainty, until the distinction between opinion and fact has disappeared entirely.

Italy and Spain approach social media with Mediterranean warmth. The algorithm here rewards community, celebration, rhythm. Your feed fills with gatherings, food, laughter, and political passion expressed as emotion rather than argument. The feedback loop feels less toxic because it is warm. Yes, people are certain about their politics, but they are certain with love. Disagreement does not destroy relationships; it is merely the spice in the conversational stew. The algorithm learns this and serves up more warmth, more connection, more reasons to feel part of something larger than yourself.

Yet even warmth can become a cage. The Mediterranean feedback loop is less about correctness and more about belonging. You engage not because you are learning but because you are affirming your place in the group. The algorithm learns this and gives you more reasons to belong, more confirmation that your tribe is right, more content that makes your people look good and their people look bad. By the time you realise you are trapped, the trap feels like home.

In Scandinavia, the feedback loop is almost invisible. Nordic users approach social media the way they approach conversation: sparingly, carefully, with minimal drama. Posts are measured, captions minimalist, outrage rare. The algorithm, bewildered by the lack of engagement, quietly moves on to louder markets. Thus the Nordic internet remains almost peaceful—proof that low emotion is the ultimate hack. Yet even there, the loop exists, humming softly beneath the calm: "You are balanced. You are sensible. Here is another article about balance for you to share responsibly."

The Scandinavian feedback loop is so gentle it is almost invisible, but it is no less powerful. People are still trapped in their own worldviews, still seeing the world through the filter of what they already believe. The difference is that they are trapped quietly, civilly, without the performative anger that characterises louder nations. The algorithm learns restraint and serves it back to them.

Across Asia, two forces collide: collective harmony and hyperconnectivity. In Japan, online disagreement feels impolite; anonymity becomes the safety valve for those who wish to express themselves uncensored. The feedback loop here is double—public politeness online and private, anonymous rage. In China, algorithms shape patriotism into performance—likes as loyalty, shares as citizenship. In Korea, digital life races at K-pop tempo: a new trend every hour, exhaustion every night. In India, conversation is democracy at full volume—millions of debates, none concluded, all simultaneously true and false.

Each Asian society has its own way of being trapped by the feedback loop. In Japan, it is the trap of politeness. In China, the trap of state-sanctioned consensus. In Korea, the trap of trend velocity. In India, the trap of infinite argument where everyone is right and nobody changes. Yet all are trapped nonetheless, fed information that reinforces what they already believe, shown connections that confirm existing relationships, given reasons to stay engaged precisely because the engagement prevents actual change.

In the Middle East, algorithms dance carefully with politics and religion. Public feeds hum with patriotism, private ones with satire. The feedback loop is double: official positivity above, subversive humour below. Even within censorship, the loop operates. People find ways to express dissent that the algorithm cannot quite detect, and the algorithm learns to tolerate certain forms of subversion while crushing others. It is a feedback loop within a feedback loop, dissent trapped within consensus, trapped within control.

In much of Africa and Latin America, social media feels younger, more alive, more hopeful than in older democracies. It is not narcissism—it is visibility long denied. The algorithm rewards joy and rhythm: dance challenges, wit, collective energy. But even celebration becomes commodity. The feedback loop feeds global curiosity whilst rarely sharing global power. The world watches and likes and shares, and the power dynamics remain unchanged. African and Latin American voices are amplified but rarely empowered. They are content, not conversation partners. The feedback loop here is particularly cruel because it masquerades as liberation.

The Psychology of the Echo

We like the loop because it loves us back. It never interrupts, never judges, never challenges our worldview. It only asks that we keep engaging. The algorithm becomes a kind of perfect friend: one that knows exactly what you want to hear and delivers it relentlessly. We mistake the algorithm's attention for empathy, its precision for understanding. But it does not know who we are; it only knows what keeps us scrolling.

We have constructed a system where disagreement is punished with invisibility and agreement is rewarded with amplification. The result is that people across the globe are increasingly living in separate information universes. Your truth and my truth are not merely different; they are mutually exclusive. We do not disagree about facts; we disagree about which facts are real. And the algorithm, perfectly indifferent to actual reality, simply amplifies whatever keeps each of us engaged in our own separate world.

The Global Conversation, Now With Subtitles

Different cultures feed the machine in their own accents:

The American says, "Look at me," and the algorithm amplifies: "Everyone look!"

The Briton says, "Do not look, but note that I exist," and the algorithm respects the irony: "Noted, with a wink."

The Frenchman says, "Observe my reasoning," and the algorithm delivers: "Here are one hundred articles proving you are right."

The Italian says, "Listen to my feelings!" and the algorithm provides: "Here are ten thousand people who feel exactly as you do!"

The Pole says, "I have seen this before," and the algorithm confirms: "You have, and it ended badly, and it will end badly again, enjoy this cynical content."

The Japanese person says "(Polite silence that the algorithm misreads as consent.)" and the algorithm provides: "Silence interpreted as engagement! More silence-adjacent content coming!"

The Nigerian says, "Watch this brilliance—then share it," and the algorithm does: "Shared to billions! Your brilliance is now content for others!"

Billions of tones, one rhythm: engagement. Billions of voices, one outcome: isolation within connection.

The Corporate Choir

Every platform sells the same hymn: connection, creativity, community. But the chorus behind it chants: data, data, data. We have built cathedrals of communication where the prayers are metrics and the gods do not answer—they analyse. The platforms do not want us to understand each other; they want us to keep clicking. They have monetised confusion, turned disagreement into engagement, and made profit the measure of all value.

We thought we were building tools for connection. We ended up building machines for isolation. We thought we were democratising voice. We ended up democratising certainty. We thought we were breaking down walls between people. We ended up building invisible walls—walls we cannot see because they are made of algorithms and recommendations and carefully curated content that shows us only what we already believe.

Cultural Remedies for the Feedback Loop

The only way out may be through cultural humility. We must learn to listen to how other cultures experience the loop, what it feels like to be trapped in their particular feedback. We must recognise that our truth is not universal, that our certainty is often just confidence born from surrounding ourselves with people who agree with us.

From the Americans: keep the optimism, lose the certainty.

From the British: keep the irony, but acknowledge what it masks.

From the French: keep the eloquence, but listen to those who cannot match your vocabulary.

From Eastern Europe: keep the realism, but recognise that cynicism can become its own trap.

From Scandinavia: keep the calm, but use it to listen rather than simply to withdraw.

From the Mediterranean: keep the passion, but notice how it can trap you as surely as apathy.

From Asia: keep the subtlety, but recognise that indirect communication can become its own form of echo chamber.

From Africa and Latin America: keep the joy, but use it to connect rather than to perform.

Conclusion: Turning Down the Echo

The Feedback Loop of Doom is not a technology problem—it is a listening problem. We have mistaken reflection for conversation, validation for connection. We have built a system that feels like the world listening to us when it is actually just us listening to ourselves at ever-increasing volume.

To break the loop, we do not need new platforms. We need an old habit: genuine curiosity. Ask one real question of someone who disagrees with you, without expecting the answer to confirm what you already believe. Listen long enough that you actually understand their position, not just the parts that offend you. Seek out disagreement not to win arguments but to actually learn something.

Every time we resist the impulse to share content that only confirms what we believe, we weaken the loop. Every time we engage with an idea we find uncomfortable, we introduce noise into the system. Every time we listen more than we speak, we begin to escape.

The feedback loop will persist. The algorithm will keep learning, keep refining, keep feeding us exactly what keeps us engaged. But perhaps, if enough of us deliberately choose to step outside it, to seek genuine connection rather than algorithmic validation, to listen rather than broadcast, something might change.

Because the most subversive act in an age of algorithms is still the same as it has always been: actually hearing someone else.

CHAPTER FOURTEEN: WHEN DID LISTENING BECOME A RADICAL ACT?

The Lost Art of Hearing Someone Else

We were told that the 21st century would be the age of information. We were assured that connectivity would break down barriers, that technology would democratise knowledge, that the world would finally understand itself through the free flow of words and ideas. It turned out to be the age of interruption. All that information, all that connectivity, all those democratised voices—and somehow we have ended up talking more and listening less. In the noise, one quiet skill has become revolutionary: the ability to listen. Not to reply, not to validate, not to perform empathy—just to hear. It should not be radical. It should be ordinary. But in a world addicted to its own echo, genuine listening now feels like rebellion.

The listener was not always a marginal figure. There was a time when listeners held genuine power. The priest, the judge, the therapist, the friend—their authority came not from speech but from silence. They absorbed stories, reflected truths, held space. They were not performers but witnesses. In many cultures, the listener was the most respected figure in the room. In Japan, the listener received more deference than the speaker. In Arab cultures, the majlis was built around the respect for listening. In African traditions, the elder who listens is honoured above the youth who speaks. To listen was to govern, to heal, to guide.

Now, the listener is an endangered species. The modern listener multitasks, scrolls, half-hears, nods on autopilot. We do not listen to understand; we listen to reload—to gather ammunition for our next point, to find the moment when we can interrupt, to locate the part of what someone is saying that relates to us. The pause between words—the sacred breathing space of understanding—has been replaced by "Yeah, totally," delivered whilst checking our phones. We perform listening the way we perform so many other things: as a gesture, not a practice. As something to get through so we can speak again.

Americans are famously friendly, famously expressive, and famously impatient. The American listener is an encourager—eyes bright, head nodding, interjecting every five seconds with "Exactly!" or "That's so true!" It is warmth, not arrogance; generosity, not ego. The intention is genuine: to make you feel seen, to validate your experience, to show that you matter. But the effect is exhausting. The American listener is so busy affirming that they are still competing for air. Real listening, by contrast, is stillness. And stillness, in America, feels almost unpatriotic—as though by not responding, you are not engaging.

The British pride themselves on listening, and in fairness, they do—silently, dryly, often with barely concealed judgement. The British listener's superpower is restraint. They let others fill the air whilst quietly evaluating. At dinner parties, they ask one question and then vanish behind their wine glass, allowing you to perform yourself into embarrassment whilst they catalogue your contradictions. It is listening as strategy—less about empathy, more about curiosity disguised as courtesy. But somewhere beneath the wit and the nodding lies the genuine virtue of patience. When a Briton truly listens, you feel safe, because they will never use your confession as content. They will file it away, remember it, and possibly use it against you years later with perfect timing and devastating irony. But not immediately. Not publicly. That is the British bargain: I listen now so I can mock later, but I mock with love.

The French do not listen; they interpret. You speak, they listen through philosophy, filter through Freud, and respond with theory. It is not dismissive—it is intellectual empathy. To them, analysing is caring. You describe your heartbreak; they explain that it is a metaphor for postmodern alienation. You share that you failed an exam; they discuss the education system's failure to account for individual learning styles. You leave either enlightened or wishing you had ordered another bottle. Listening in France is cerebral rather than emotional: a duel of understanding rather than a hug. But at least they are paying attention. At least they are not scrolling.

Scandinavia operates according to entirely different principles. In Scandinavia, listening is a civic virtue, something to be taken seriously and practiced deliberately. People wait for others to finish—not because they were trained to, but because it is inconceivable to do otherwise. To interrupt would be violence. Meetings contain vast meadows of silence in which thought grows slowly, where people think before they speak, where reflection is more valued than reactivity. A Swedish friend once told me, "We listen until the room feels ready for words again." It is almost mystical, this idea that silence has a readiness, that there is a precise moment when listening becomes speech. The still listener does not nod or murmur; they attend. When they finally speak, the room exhales.

In Warsaw or Prague, listeners are pragmatic. They do not perform emotion; they absorb facts. Their version of empathy sounds like advice: "So what will you do about it?" It is not impatience—it is cultural triage. When life has been unpredictable for generations, when systems have consistently failed populations, people learn to hear what matters and discard what does not. You can tell an Eastern European has listened because they remember. They will not flood you with comfort; they will bring it up three months later when it counts. They will say, "Remember when you told me about that thing? I have been thinking about it." And suddenly, you realise that whilst you were speaking, they were actually listening—not performing listening, but genuinely receiving what you said.

In Italy, Spain, and Greece, everyone listens—while talking. It is not disrespect; it is duet. You speak, they echo, amplify, anticipate. It feels chaotic to outsiders but alive within its rhythm. The Mediterranean listener interrupts not to dominate but to show belonging. "Sì, sì, exactly!" they cry, half-rising from their chair. You finish your story breathless, but somehow understood. The listener has matched your rhythm, added their own experience, made your story part of the collective narrative. You do not feel heard so much as you feel incorporated.

In the Arab world, listening is generosity. To let someone speak without interruption is to honour their soul. The host listens with eyes, posture, and patience. Stories are heard in full, digested, and only then discussed. You are not hurried. Your words are given the dignity of time. It is empathy expressed through hospitality—the art of making silence feel warm. Even heated debate maintains this structure: passion within boundaries, conviction expressed through courtesy. The listener is not a passive recipient but an active participant in the act of honouring another person's existence.

Across East and Southeast Asia, listening is not a soft skill but a moral one. It signals discipline, respect, maturity. In Japan, a listener's silence communicates attention; in China, their minimal responses show concentration. To interrupt is to imply superiority; to listen is to preserve harmony. In India, the listener is also storyteller-in-waiting. They listen with compassion, but the moment you stop, they will match you with a tale of their own—a kind of conversational karma, a recognition that listening is reciprocal, that your story needs my story to be complete. In all, Asian listening balances humility with reciprocity.

In many African cultures, listening is a shared act. People gather to hear stories, songs, and news together. Understanding arises through rhythm and repetition—call and response. The listener is participant, not spectator. They hum, nod, echo key phrases—acknowledging presence without interruption. In some traditions, the greatest insult is to walk away before a story ends. Listening is respect, and respect is identity. To listen is to say: you matter, your story matters, and I am willing to sit with you in this moment for as long as it takes.

Modern technology has rewired the human ear in ways that are only beginning to be understood. We listen to sound, not speech. Podcasts, audiobooks, background chatter—we consume voices without connection. The "listener" today is multitasking, distracted, transactional. The screen talks; we pretend to hear. Every "heard" notification is a technological lie. We hear everything, but we listen to nothing. The distinction is crucial: hearing is passive reception; listening is active engagement. We have optimised for hearing and eliminated listening almost entirely.

Why is listening so difficult? Because listening is surrender. It requires humility, patience, curiosity—the very traits the modern ego avoids. When we truly listen, we risk being changed. That is terrifying. So we nod sympathetically whilst formulating our next post. We are not afraid of other people's voices. We are afraid of losing our own certainty. Listening means admitting that our view might be incomplete, that the other person might have insight we lack, that their experience is as valid as ours. These are radical admissions in a culture that worships confidence.

Each culture has developed its own relationship with listening, and these differences reveal what each society values. The American listener's interruptions reveal a culture that values engagement and enthusiasm. The British listener's silence reveals a culture that values discretion and observation. The French listener's analysis reveals a culture that values intellect. The Scandinavian listener's patience reveals a culture that values deliberation. The Eastern European listener's pragmatism reveals a culture that values survival. The Mediterranean listener's participation reveals a culture that values connection. The Asian listener's discipline reveals a culture that values harmony. The Arab listener's hospitality reveals a culture that values dignity. The African listener's communalism reveals a culture that values belonging.

What unites them all, despite their differences, is that genuine listening has become rarer everywhere. The noise of the modern world—the notifications, the feeds, the constant demand for response—has eroded the capacity to listen across all cultures. We have all become slightly deaf to each other, not from biological failing but from cultural choice.

The Psychology of Presence

When we listen genuinely, something remarkable happens. We disappear. Not in the sense of being erased, but in the sense of stepping back from the centre. The ego quiets. The agenda dissolves. What remains is pure attention. This is why listening feels so radical—it requires a kind of death of self, a temporary suspension of our own importance. For creatures as narcissistic as humans, this is terrifying.

Yet every human who has experienced genuine listening knows how transformative it is. To be truly heard—not judged, not advised, not immediately related to someone else's experience—is one of the most healing things that can happen. It is why therapy works, why confession still exists, why people will tell strangers on trains things they have never told their closest friends. In the presence of genuine listening, something opens. Truth becomes possible.

Cultural Remedies for the Deaf Age

From Scandinavia: Honour the pause; it is where wisdom lives. Create silence deliberately and defend it fiercely.

From Japan: Let silence speak before you do. Respect ma—the space between things. It contains meaning.

From Eastern Europe: Listen for what is unsaid. The gaps in conversation often contain the most important truths.

From the Middle East: Use pauses to confer dignity on the speaker. Silence is a form of respect.

From Africa: Share the act of hearing. Listening is communal; it is how we belong to each other.

From the Mediterranean: Listen with emotion, but do so with presence, not performance. Your interruptions can be love, but only if you are actually present.

From Britain: Listen with restraint. Do not need to respond immediately. Let what someone has said settle before you speak.

From France: Listen critically, but listen. Your analysis is valuable, but only if you have actually heard what needs to be analysed.

From America: Listen without needing to fix. Not everything that is shared needs to be solved. Sometimes people just need to be heard.

From Asia: Listen with humility. Understand that the other person's knowledge is as valid as yours. Harmony requires hearing.

The Future of Listening

The future of civilisation may depend on rediscovering how to listen. Not to respond faster, not to build empathy brands for corporate marketing, but to rebuild the most basic human capacity: to hear another person. Because listening is the last unautomated human act. It cannot be coded, scaled, or monetised. It is simply presence, freely given.

When we relearn that—whether in a Swedish boardroom, a Cairo café, a Mexican kitchen, or a London pub—the world might, for the first time in decades, start making sense again. Not because we will agree about everything, but because we will finally understand what everyone is actually saying. We will hear the fear beneath the anger, the hope beneath the cynicism, the longing beneath the indifference.

Conclusion: The Sound of Understanding

In the end, listening is not a skill to be developed so much as a capacity to be recovered. We all knew how to do it once. Children listen with absolute attention. Animals listen with their entire being. Some cultures have never forgotten. It is only modern Western industrial societies that have decided listening is optional, that distraction is acceptable, that performance is sufficient.

The rediscovery of listening may be the most important conversational skill of the coming decades. Not the silence of avoidance or awkwardness, but the silence of presence. The silence that says: I am listening so carefully that I need time to process what you are saying. The silence that creates space for others to think completely. The silence that acknowledges complexity too deep for quick answers.

Because after all the words, after all the arguments and broadcasts and performances, after all the noise and the feedback loops and the aggressive agreement, the most eloquent line in any conversation might still be the one no one utters. The pause where understanding happens. The silence where meaning lives. The space where, if we are very quiet, very still, and very brave, we might actually hear one another.

And if we can hear one another, perhaps we can finally begin to speak to one another.

CHAPTER FIFTEEN: THE POWER POSE AND THE VERBAL FLEX

How Confidence Learned to Speak Every Language

Once, power spoke softly. The authority of age, wisdom, or legitimate position did not require volume. A quiet word from someone respected carried weight that a thousand shouts could never match. Now power shouts, stands wide, and holds eye contact until you submit. We live in an age where confidence has been mistaken for competence, where posture has become a form of proof, and where the body is understood as a résumé. The voice is its soundtrack, and together they perform a global dance of dominance that varies by culture but speaks the same underlying language: I am certain, therefore I am right.

Every culture teaches its own dialect of dominance, but as global business, social media, and self-help seminars have merged into a single cultural soup, a universal language of swagger has begun to emerge—part TED Talk, part yoga class, part gladiator arena. Hands steepled. Chest open. Voice low and measured. Smile calibrated to suggest both warmth and authority. This is not communication; it is choreography. It is the performance of power so perfected that we have forgotten it is a performance at all.

In the United States, confidence is civic duty. Children are raised with the explicit instruction to "use your voice," to "project positivity," and to "fake it till you make it." The result is a culture where volume equals virtue and where confidence is treated as a commodity that can be manufactured, performed, and eventually believed. The Power Pose is standard issue in American corporate culture: shoulders back, hands visible on the table or gesturing expansively, eye contact unbroken by doubt or modesty. Add a deep-voiced "Here is the thing..." and you can sell anything from life insurance to lunar colonisation to your own complete incompetence. The Verbal Flex is relentless optimism, enthusiasm as persuasion, positivity deployed like a weapon.

"I am so excited about this!" The sentence could introduce a merger or a muffin recipe; the tone remains identical. The American businessman or businesswoman learns that conviction matters more than correctness, that the appearance of certainty is more valuable than actual certainty. This relentless optimism can be exhausting to outsiders but intoxicating to Americans. It is, after all, the nation that turned self-belief into its leading export. Every innovation, every company, every revolution begins with an American saying "This will work," with complete confidence and partial information.

Britain performs power differently: through understatement. The Power Pose is replaced by posture denial—slouching aristocratically, one hand in pocket, expression of faint amusement suggesting that dominance is beneath consideration. The authority conveyed is not "I am powerful" but rather "I could dominate this conversation, but I am choosing not to because I am above it." The Verbal Flex here is irony—that quiet weapon of superiority. A simple "Right" or "Quite" can end an argument, terminate a meeting, or demolish a marriage proposal. It is authority disguised as indifference. The British do not project confidence; they ration it, distribute it carefully, make it seem accidental rather than performed.

The British Power Pose says: I am comfortable enough with my authority that I do not need to prove it. This is deeply effective in British contexts where overt display is considered vulgar. But it confuses outsiders who are waiting for something more explicit. The American reads British understatement as uncertainty; the Brit reads American enthusiasm as insecurity. Both are performing confidence, but they are speaking different dialects of the same language.

French authority is aesthetic. The stance is relaxed yet deliberate; the gestures minimal but meaningful. The voice, smooth and measured, carries centuries of intellectual confidence. The Power Pose here is poise—head tilted slightly, eyes half-narrowed, as though considering whether your argument is art or error. There is something almost seductive about it. The Verbal Flex is precision: the ability to quote Baudelaire without sounding pretentious, to make complex ideas sound simple, to marshal language so elegantly that disagreement feels barbaric. In France, power is not loudness but linguistic grace. A well-constructed sentence can be more persuasive than a thousand shouts.

The French have understood something that most cultures are still learning: that in a society that worships eloquence, the most confident person in the room is often the one who speaks least but most carefully. Silence here is not weakness; it is strategy. When everyone else is talking, the person who pauses, considers, and speaks only when they have something perfect to say commands the room.

In Eastern Europe, power arrives through stillness. Arms crossed, gaze unwavering, tone calm to the point of chilling. The Power Pose here says: I have survived worse than this meeting, worse than this conversation, worse than your attempt to intimidate me. It is not aggression but endurance made visible. The Verbal Flex is deadpan truth. No slogans, no smiles, no softening of reality—just statements carved from granite.

When an Eastern European says, "It will be difficult," they mean the apocalypse is en route and you should prepare accordingly. Confidence in this region does not need rehearsal; it is inherited from grandparents who negotiated with history itself.

There is something almost refreshing about Eastern European confidence. It does not perform; it simply is. The person standing quietly, saying little, radiating the certainty of someone who has seen worse, becomes the most credible person in the room. In cultures obsessed with youth and performance, this quiet authority born from survival stands out as genuinely powerful.

In Scandinavia, the Power Pose is an act of anti-theatre. Feet grounded, gestures small, voice even. Everything about Nordic confidence suggests that you do not need to prove anything; the proof is in the performance of not performing. The Verbal Flex is brevity. A Swede can demolish a verbose American simply by saying, "I see your point," and nothing else. The silence that follows is power distilled to its essence. In egalitarian societies where overt dominance is frowned upon, quiet certainty becomes the ultimate form of authority. It says: I know what I am talking about, and I do not need to convince you because the truth will eventually reveal itself.

This Nordic confidence is terrifying to those accustomed to American enthusiasm or French eloquence. There is no spectacle, no performance, no seduction. Just the calm certainty that what you have said is either correct or incorrect, and time will tell which.

In Italy and Spain, the Power Pose is kinetic. Hips, hands, eyebrows—everything participates in the performance of confidence. To speak without gesturing would be an insult to emotion and an abandonment of self-expression. The Italian Verbal Flex is poetry disguised as conversation: rhythm, repetition, exaggeration deployed with such skill that disagreement becomes almost impossible. In Spain, confidence comes with volume and melody; disagreement is expressed in major key. What outsiders read as chaos is actually choreography—emotion as eloquence, passion as persuasion.

Dominance here is not cold authority but charismatic warmth. You do not yield because you are silenced; you yield because you are dazzled. The Italian or Spanish speaker makes confidence look like joy, and who wants to argue against joy?

In the Middle East, power is expressed through dignity. The Power Pose is upright, still, controlled; gestures minimal, voice resonant and deep. Authority speaks slowly and looks directly—not to intimidate, but to honour. The Verbal Flex lies in eloquence. To speak beautifully is to lead. A well-turned phrase can outshine a hierarchy; a poetic digression can carry more weight than a direct order. This is power expressed through artistry rather than aggression. It is confidence born from understanding that real authority does not shout; it whispers in perfect Arabic.

Across Asia, overt display is often replaced by calibrated grace. The Power Pose is composure; the Verbal Flex, subtle emphasis. In Japan, bowing is both humility and control—lowering oneself to elevate one's status through discipline. The person who can bow deepest is the strongest. In China, confidence is collective: the ability to speak as "we," not "I." Individual confidence is actually seen as weakness; collective confidence is power. In India, the verbal flex is fluency—switching between English and local languages as proof of intellect and reach. The Asian art of confidence lies in equilibrium: presence without pressure, strength without show.

In much of Africa, power still speaks through rhythm. The body aligns with voice; gesture follows story. It is oratory, not performance. The Power Pose is grounded, feet firm, shoulders wide—signalling steadiness. The Verbal Flex is cadence: a speaker who can make a crowd sway without raising volume, who can make silence feel like participation, who can make everyone in the room feel like they are part of something larger than themselves. Confidence here is not about self; it is about community resonance. The leader is the one whose words feel like belonging.

The Global Theatre of Power

Put them all together—the American pep, the British drawl, the French poise, the Eastern European stare, the Mediterranean opera, the Nordic calm, the Asian grace, the African rhythm—and you have humanity's greatest collaboration: the performance of confidence. We have learned to posture across borders. Global capitalism, international conferences, and social media have created a new species: Homo Assertivus—fluent in body language, tone, and self-belief. Every culture has learned to perform confidence, and the only universal taboo is now hesitation.

Walk into any international meeting and observe. The American is performing enthusiasm. The Brit is performing indifference. The Swede is performing calm. The Italian is performing passion. The German is performing precision. The Frenchman is performing eloquence. The Eastern European is performing endurance. Everyone is performing something, and everyone is convinced their performance is simply authenticity.

But what if the entire enterprise is camouflage? What if confidence and competence correlate far less than we believe? The studies suggest they do. The loud person often leads, but the quiet person often fixes. The Power Pose wins the room; the listener saves it later. We trust charisma because it feels decisive, not because it is correct. The most confident person in the room is not necessarily the most competent. They are often just the most committed to their own mythology.

Yet confidence matters. It matters because people respond to it. It matters because decisions are made by those who seem certain. It matters because the world runs on the decisions of confident people, for better or worse. The question is not whether to project confidence—everyone does—but what kind of confidence to project.

The Confidence Illusion

There is a dangerous gap between confidence and competence. We have built systems that reward the former whilst hoping the latter will follow. We elect confident politicians, hire confident executives, follow confident entrepreneurs. Yet confidence is merely conviction, and conviction is merely a state of mind. It does not predict accuracy. It does not ensure wisdom. A confident fool is still a fool, just louder.

The problem is that we have become so focused on the performance of confidence that we have forgotten to ask whether the person actually knows what they are talking about. We have mistaken certainty for correctness so thoroughly that nuance has been driven nearly to extinction. In a world where power comes to those who seem most certain, humility becomes a liability. Doubt becomes dangerous. Questions become weakness.

Yet some of the most important decisions in human history have been made by people willing to sit with uncertainty, to acknowledge doubt, to admit that they did not know. The scientist who says "I do not know, but let us find out together" is actually more powerful than the one who declares certainty. The leader who admits error is actually more credible than the one who performs infallibility. But these people rarely rise to positions of power because they lack the confident performance that gets people elected or promoted.

Cultural Remedies for the Confidence Crisis

What each culture needs to learn from the others:

From America: keep the optimism, rediscover doubt. Confidence is useful, but it is not the same as knowledge.

From Britain: keep the irony, risk sincerity. Your understatement is elegant, but sometimes things need to be said plainly.

From France: keep the elegance, accept imperfection. Perfection is the enemy of progress.

From Germany: keep the precision, soften the delivery. Correctness matters, but so does connection.

From Eastern Europe: keep the endurance, add hope. You have survived, and survival is impressive, but so is believing things might improve.

From Scandinavia: keep the calm, allow pride. Confidence is not arrogance; it is simply the acknowledgement of competence.

From the Mediterranean: keep the passion, listen more. Your enthusiasm is contagious, but it can also prevent you from hearing.

From Asia: keep the discipline, invite play. Restraint is wise, but so is spontaneity.

From Africa: keep the rhythm, invite others to dance. Your cadence is powerful, but power is only real if it is shared.

Conclusion: The Quiet Power

Real confidence is not the absence of doubt; it is the decision to continue with it. The truly self-assured person can say, "I do not know," and still command respect. Because certainty dominates; curiosity inspires. And in a world where everyone is shouting "Back to Me!" with their Power Pose and Verbal Flex, the quietest voice might still be the bravest.

The next evolution of confidence may not look like a pose at all. It may be stillness, listening, the confidence to not perform. Real power does not need to flex; it needs to understand. It is not the stance or the sound that persuades—it is the space one makes for others to stand tall too. Because in the end, posture fades, tone softens, and every performance ends the same way: with

QUENTIN DRUMMOND ANDERSON

silence, and the question—

Did anyone actually hear?

CHAPTER SIXTEEN: THE POLITICS OF TALK

When Nations Argue Like People

Every country has its national conversation style—the way it debates, disagrees, and performs conviction on the public stage. Watch any parliament or press conference long enough and you can discern it immediately: politics is just conversation with microphones, suits, and considerably higher stakes. It is all there in the political sphere—the interrupters and the humblebrags, the aggressive agreeers and the name-droppers, the Pub Philosophers and the Dinner-Table Diplomats. The only difference between a parliamentary debate and a heated pub argument is the wardrobe, the expense account, and the fact that one might actually determine the course of nations whilst the other merely determines who buys the next round.

Politics today sounds less like dialogue and more like an audition. Every leader performs a tone designed to soothe their home audience whilst infuriating everyone else. Diplomacy has become duelling monologues—simultaneous declarations interrupted by translators who are themselves unsure what has actually been agreed. The 24-hour news cycle provides the lighting, social media supplies the chorus, and voters serve as reluctant spectators shouting "Mute!" at their screens whilst the performance continues regardless.

We used to say "actions speak louder than words." In modern politics, words are the action. Speech has become the primary currency of power. The ability to control the narrative, to frame the debate, to dominate the conversation—these are now more important than policy itself. A well-delivered lie beats a poorly-articulated truth. A confident wrong answer beats a hesitant right one. The person who can sound most certain wins, regardless of whether their certainty is warranted.

The United States runs on rhetoric like a car runs on petrol. The national faith in free speech has produced a culture where silence looks suspicious and verbosity heroic. American politics is a performance of conviction that would make theatre critics weep. Every senator speaks as though auditioning for Mr. Smith Goes to Washington. Every governor uses "folks" as punctuation, invoking the common person whilst standing in rooms that common people will never enter. Every debate is a sermon disguised as conversation, every policy proposal a morality play.

American populism is pure "Back to Me" culture in patriotic costume. Each candidate promises to "listen to the people," and then immediately begins a podcast. The irony is lost on nobody, yet the performance continues because it works. Americans believe that words can change the world, that if you say something loudly enough and often enough, it becomes true. This is not entirely cynicism—there is genuine idealism in this belief. But it has metastasised into a political system where rhetoric has entirely replaced substance.

The American political speech follows a formula so predictable it could be written by algorithm. Begin with a personal anecdote. Move into a list of grievances. Propose a solution that is simultaneously vague and grandiose. Invoke the founding fathers or contemporary heroes. Build to a crescendo of patriotic language. End with a call to action that requires nothing specific but everything emotional. The crowd cheers. Nothing changes. But everyone feels like something has been said, and in American politics, the feeling matters more than the reality.

In Britain, politics is theatre with hecklers and more refined insults. The House of Commons remains the world's most eloquent shouting match: half-Oxford Union debate society, half rugby scrum with parliamentary procedure. Here, interruption is not just permitted; it is etiquette. Members rise to shout "Hear, hear!" and "Order!" with the musicality of birds defending territory. The ritual is so established that it has become almost performative—everyone knows the dance, everyone plays their part, and somehow, despite the apparent chaos, government continues.

British politicians perform intelligence through wit. The deadlier the quip, the higher the poll numbers. Prime Minister's Questions is less government and more game show, where the leader who can deliver the most cutting remark wins the day. It is conversation as combat, yet somehow civility survives beneath the noise. Like the British dinner party, it is chaos wrapped in charm, where you can tell someone they are an absolute fool, provided you do it with sufficient elegance and a well-timed pause.

The British political style assumes an educated audience capable of understanding subtext and irony. The politician who needs to explain the joke has lost. The one who can deliver a cutting remark and move on without elaboration wins. This works beautifully for audiences raised in British culture but confuses foreigners who are waiting for something more explicit. The American reads British political rhetoric as evasive; the Brit reads American explicitness as crude. Both are right, from their own perspective.

In France, politics is an ongoing philosophical debate occasionally interrupted by elections. Leaders quote Rousseau before breakfast and Descartes before declaring war. To speak well is to rule. The French politician's speech is a work of art: rhetorical flourishes, existential digressions, at least one reference to liberty, and preferably a mention of France's role in defending civilisation. Language is not merely the vehicle for ideas; it is the idea itself. A poorly-constructed sentence is a sign of poorly-constructed thought.

But eloquence cuts both ways. When the people protest, they do it with slogans as poetic as the speeches they oppose. The barricade is the French reply to a bad paragraph. In France, the national conversation is constant and combustible—words as revolution, round two hundred and counting. French politics assumes its citizens are intellectuals capable of engaging in philosophical debate. The government that cannot argue its position in elegant language does not deserve to govern.

Germany values precision and process. Every speech is an engineering project—carefully measured, structurally sound, slightly humourless. The Power Pose is replaced by Power Grammar. Every word is chosen for accuracy. Every sentence is constructed for clarity. The tone is serious, the phrasing cautious. Even applause feels procedural. German politicians do not inspire; they inform. They do not seduce; they convince through logic. The result? A nation that sounds sober, reliable, and occasionally allergic to spontaneity. German political rhetoric may lack charisma, but it compensates with comprehension. No one leaves a Bundestag debate confused about what was said, even if they disagree with it.

In Eastern Europe, political speech bears the weight of history. Decades of propaganda have taught people to decode tone faster than content. The region's politicians oscillate between defiant oratory and weary pragmatism. The Romanian politician shouts reform; the Polish one quotes scripture and history; the Hungarian declares destiny. To outsiders it may sound theatrical, but to locals it is familiar: rhetoric as defence mechanism. They have seen ideologies rise and fall; they have learned to listen for what is missing rather than what is said. Every speech carries an undertone of irony—We have heard it all before, and it rarely ends well.

Eastern European politics is characterised by an almost tragic realism. The speeches are passionate, but the passion is tinged with doubt. The declarations are bold, but the boldness is tempered by memory. There is an understanding that words matter less than power, that rhetoric is necessary but ultimately hollow, that the real decisions are made in rooms where no one is speaking loudly.

In Scandinavia, the political tone is so calm it feels medicinal. Leaders speak in consensus; parliaments hum rather than roar. The goal is not dominance but agreement. The Prime Minister addresses the nation as though explaining IKEA assembly instructions: clearly, carefully, without drama. Even scandal feels gentle in Scandinavian politics. The politician who loses their temper has already lost the debate. The one who remains calm, collected, and slightly bored by the entire proceeding maintains power.

This quiet confidence confuses louder nations but comforts citizens. It sounds like democracy functioning too smoothly to trend, like government that is competent enough that it does not need to shout about its competence. Scandinavian political rhetoric assumes citizens are rational and will respond to reason. It does not appeal to emotion because it trusts that logic is sufficient. Whether this is true or merely a reflection of cultural values is debatable, but the results speak for themselves: functional societies, low corruption, and politicians who seem to actually believe in the institutions they serve.

In Italy, Spain, and Greece, politics is theatre without script. Parliaments resemble family dinners where everyone talks, no one listens, and somehow decisions get made. It is passion, not policy, that wins the room. Debate here is music—crescendos of outrage followed by hugs, coffee, and more debate. The Italian parliament's decibel level could power a small city. The Spanish opposition interrupts with applause. Greek politicians quote Homer and shout like Spartans defending Thermopylae.

It is chaos, but democratic chaos—at least everyone gets a solo. The assumption is that all citizens are emotionally intelligent enough to understand that passionate disagreement does not mean personal hostility. You can argue fiercely about government policy and still embrace your opponent at the end of the day. The political style reflects this: high drama, high volume, high emotion, yet somehow functional government emerges from the noise.

In much of the Middle East, politics remains an art of formality and oratory. The tone is respectful, poetic, steeped in metaphor and historical reference. A leader's speech must balance strength with grace, pride with piety. Even dissent carries decorum; criticism is delivered through parable, satire, or silence. But beneath the ceremony lies fierce conviction. When voices rise, they rise with centuries of rhythm behind them. Politics here is still public poetry—the oldest kind of power.

The assumption is that citizens understand layers of meaning, that what is said literally is less important than what is implied, that the music of language matters as much as its content. A speech is not judged by what it says but by how beautifully it says it.

Across Asia, politics tends towards restraint. Leaders speak slowly, formally, often reading statements crafted with surgical precision. The tone projects stability rather than charisma. In Japan, a single misplaced phrase can end a career; in China, language is a tool of order; speech defines loyalty. In India, meanwhile, politics has become a festival of oratory— half cinema, half sermon, all spectacle. Across the continent, confidence remains collective: "We," not "I." It is the politics of harmony—and when it cracks, the noise is deafening.

In much of Africa and Latin America, politics belongs to the street as much as the parliament. Leaders must speak with rhythm, emotion, and authenticity—not because it is fashionable, but because it is survival. In Lagos, speeches sound like sermons; in Buenos Aires, like tango lyrics. Power flows through oratory that feels communal, almost musical. Even protest chants have cadence—democracy as drumbeat, resistance as rhythm.

The Digital Parliament

Social media has turned every citizen into a politician and every comment thread into a miniature parliament. The new rule: whoever types last wins. The populist and the influencer now share the same toolkit—charisma, outrage, brevity, and strategic lighting. Policy is announced in hashtags. Diplomacy happens in memes. Politics has finally caught up with the rest of us: it is all "Back to Me," all the time, just with more followers and higher stakes.

The Global Feedback Loop

In truth, every nation's political style is its conversational DNA magnified. America interrupts, so American politics is constant interruption. Britain deflects, so British politics is constant deflection. France debates, so French politics is constant debate. Eastern Europe endures, so Eastern European politics is constant endurance. Scandinavia mediates, so Scandinavian politics is constant mediation. The Mediterranean gesticulates, so Mediterranean politics is constant gesture. Asia balances, so Asian politics is constant balancing act. Africa unites, so African politics is constant unity-building exercise.

The great irony? All are convinced that their way is the voice of reason. The American believes that loud declaration is clarity. The Brit believes that irony is wisdom. The Frenchman believes that eloquence is truth. The Eastern European believes that cynicism is realism. The Swede believes that calm is correctness. The Italian believes that passion is authenticity. The Asian believes that restraint is respect. The African believes that unity is justice.

And they are all right, from within their own systems. The

tragedy is that when these different conversational styles collide on the international stage, nothing gets resolved. We have a world where every nation is performing its own national conversation style, convinced of its superiority, incapable of hearing anything else.

Cultural Lessons from the Political Stage

From the U.S.: conviction matters—but stop talking long enough to test whether it is correct.

From Britain: wit wins crowds, but it does not win wars. Eventually, substance matters.

From France: elegance persuades, but only when paired with empathy. Beauty without humanity is just decoration.

From Eastern Europe: history humbles hubris. Remember that your idea has probably been tried before.

From Scandinavia: calm is not weakness. Sometimes the person who refuses to shout is actually the strongest.

From the Mediterranean: passion is power, but chaos has a cost. Enthusiasm must eventually produce results.

From Asia: discipline preserves dignity. Restraint is not the same as weakness.

From Africa and Latin America: authenticity transcends rhetoric. The person who speaks from the heart is often heard louder than the one who speaks from the script.

Conclusion: From Shouting to Speaking

Politics will always reflect its people. When conversation becomes performance, governments become theatre. When listening returns, democracy does too. The healthiest nations may not be the loudest or the cleverest—but the ones still capable of silence between sentences, still capable of changing their minds, still capable of admitting when they do not know.

Whether in a parliament, a café, or a dinner party, the same rule applies: The world changes not when someone speaks—but when someone finally listens. And the politician, like the person, who can listen without immediately planning their response, who can sit with disagreement without feeling threatened by it, who can admit uncertainty without losing authority—that person, in any language, in any culture, is the one worth following.

Because real leadership is not about having all the answers. It is about asking the right questions and actually hearing the answers.

CHAPTER SEVENTEEN: THE CONSPIRACY OF CLEVERNESS

Why Everyone Sounds Brilliant and Nobody Feels Understood

Intelligence was once a private virtue. A person of learning kept their knowledge close, deployed it judiciously, and allowed their competence to speak for itself through action rather than declaration. Now it has become a social accessory —worn, flaunted, hashtagged, and monetised. We used to hide our cleverness to avoid appearing arrogant. Now we parade it to avoid seeming irrelevant. It is not that the world has become smarter. It is that cleverness has become a competition sport—the global Olympics of overthinking, where everyone is competing to demonstrate their intelligence whilst simultaneously preventing anyone from actually learning anything.

We live in a civilisation obsessed with intellectual display. Everyone has opinions, platforms, credentials, and a podcast. The internet democratised information and, with it, delusion: every comment section now hosts a symposium of people convinced of their own expertise. The problem is not ignorance —it is performance. We do not think to understand anymore. We think to appear as though we understand. We confuse articulation with insight, verbosity with depth, confidence with knowledge. Welcome to the Conspiracy of Cleverness: a world where insight has been replaced by inference, where curiosity has been replaced by commentary, where the ability to sound intelligent has become more valuable than actually being intelligent.

The New Smart Arms Race

Modern technology has industrialised intellect. We have created systems that reward the performance of thinking without requiring actual thought. LinkedIn thought pieces, bite-sized philosophy threads, AI-generated wisdom, TikTok explanations of complex concepts—all curated to signal thoughtfulness without requiring thought. The TED Talk became the new sermon: fifteen minutes to enlightenment, packaged attractively, easily shareable, requiring nothing of the listener except to feel like they have learned something. We applaud, we share, we move on—enlightened for precisely the length of a WiFi signal before scrolling to the next bite of wisdom.

Cleverness has become the influencer's halo, the politician's shield, the executive's currency. It is no longer a quality to develop quietly; it is a brand to build publicly. Every thought must be tweeted, every insight must be published, every observation must be turned into content. The result is a world drowning in commentary where actual understanding has become almost invisible because it does not perform well. A nuanced analysis will lose to a catchy oversimplification every single time. A careful argument will be outpaced by a confident assertion. A question will be buried beneath a thousand answers.

In America, cleverness is extroverted and evangelistic. The American intellectual does not brood—they brand. Ideas are TED Talks, think pieces, LinkedIn essays, motivational mantras. Even humility is curated: "Here is what failure taught me about success." Knowledge is a form of hustle. You do not read to learn; you read to lead. You do not understand to grow; you understand to build your personal brand. American cleverness is entrepreneurial: intellect that sells itself with a smile, that knows how to market wisdom as though it were a start-up. The assumption is that if you can explain it compellingly enough, you understand it well enough. This is dangerously false.

The American version of the conspiracy of cleverness is perhaps the most visible because it is so thoroughly commercialised. Every university is a business, every podcast a potential revenue stream, every intellectual a potential influencer. The result is that American intellectualism has become increasingly focused on what sells rather than what is true. The conspiracy is not malicious—it is structural. The system rewards performance, so performers dominate. Those who are actually thinking, quietly and carefully, about complex problems without immediate application to social media engagement, are increasingly marginalised.

Britain is allergic to overt cleverness. It hides genius behind jokes, depth behind understatement. To sound too intelligent is to risk social death. So the British intellectual has learned to disguise brilliance as bumbling charm. The archetype is the Oxford wit, half self-deprecating, half devastatingly brilliant. A British intellectual will puncture a profound point with "but what do I know?" right after you realise they know everything. It is intellect in camouflage—deadly, elegant, and wrapped in irony so tight that outsiders sometimes miss the point entirely.

The British conspiracy of cleverness is less obvious than the American version because it is performed through what appears to be humility. The person who says "I probably should not say this, but..." is about to say something brilliant and knows it. The one who begins with "This is probably wrong, but..." is actually quite certain of their correctness. It is intellectual modesty as a performative strategy, and it is remarkably effective. The British get to display their intelligence whilst maintaining plausible deniability about doing so. They can seem both humble and brilliant simultaneously—a trick that confuses Americans and impresses other Europeans.

In France, intellect is erotic. Conversation is foreplay; philosophy, flirtation. To be clever is to be desirable—provided you make it sound poetic. The tone is confident, never apologetic: "Je pense, donc je séduis." French cleverness has rhythm. It dances through contradiction, quoting Camus with the same ease as gossip. Even café debates about WiFi have existential undertones. France is the only nation where you can sound profound ordering a sandwich, and the Conspiracy of Cleverness here is that everyone participates in this performance willingly. To be French is to be intellectually pretentious; to admit this would be to break the spell.

The French version of the conspiracy is perhaps the most beautiful because it is pursued with such commitment to form. The idea is less important than how beautifully it is expressed. A poorly-reasoned argument delivered with eloquence will win over a correct argument delivered plainly. This has its charms —it produces beautiful literature and elegant philosophy—but it also means that France has perfected the art of sounding intelligent whilst saying nothing particularly useful.

In Germany, cleverness is a discipline. Logic replaces performance, structure replaces charm. A German intellectual does not need to speak loudly—their reasoning does the shouting. They dismantle ideas the way they might disassemble a carburettor: with precision, with grim satisfaction, with the certainty that the correct answer exists and can be found through rigorous application of thought. The Verbal Flex here is thoroughness. To be vague is to be dishonest. To be ironic is to be unclear. To be clear is to be virtuous.

German cleverness assumes that truth is discoverable and that language's job is to communicate it accurately. There is no room for decoration or performance. The conspiracy of cleverness in Germany is actually a conspiracy for clarity—the belief that if you think clearly enough and speak clearly enough, you will be understood. This is admirable but sometimes naive. It assumes that all disagreement stems from misunderstanding, when sometimes it stems from genuinely different values or interests.

In Eastern Europe, cleverness is survival. A mix of melancholy, irony, and brutal realism shaped by centuries of unreliable authority. Here, intellect is less display and more defence. People speak in aphorisms, dark jokes, and metaphors sharp enough to cut through censorship. The Polish or Czech intellectual does not say, "I think." They say, "It is obvious," and you feel both enlightened and vaguely scolded. Cleverness here is defiance disguised as despair—the poetry of people too intelligent to believe the propaganda, and too proud to stop talking anyway.

The Eastern European conspiracy of cleverness is unique because it does not aspire to universal truths. It is cynical enough to know that all grand claims are suspect, yet intelligent enough to articulate why. The result is a kind of brilliant resignation: clever observation of the futility of cleverness itself. It is meta-intelligence, so to speak—intelligence that understands its own limitations and limitations of all thought.

In Scandinavia, cleverness whispers. There is even a cultural law against intellectual arrogance: the Jantelagen—the idea that no one is better than anyone else. A Swedish or Danish intellectual speaks simply, pauses often, and never shows off. Knowledge is communal, not competitive. If an American genius says, "I have a vision," the Nordic one says, "We have an idea." It is intellect as collective wisdom—a calm antidote to the world's shouting match. The conspiracy of cleverness in Scandinavia is actually a conspiracy against cleverness: the belief that intelligence is best expressed through restraint and that the truly intelligent person is the one who does not need to prove it.

The Mediterranean approaches intelligence with rhythm and drama. An Italian philosopher does not write papers; they perform them. A Spanish intellectual does not persuade; they enchant. A Greek scholar still argues like Plato—except now the amphitheatre is a café. It is intellect with rhythm, drama, and espresso. A verbal opera where cleverness is not cold—it is alive, it moves, it touches the heart as much as the mind. The conspiracy here is that emotion and intellect are not opposites but partners. Feeling deeply is a form of thinking deeply.

In the Arab world, intellect retains its sacred aura. Knowledge is inheritance—the continuation of wisdom from poets, prophets, and philosophers. To speak beautifully is to think morally. To quote poetry is to show not just learning but lineage. The Middle Eastern intellectual speaks with gravitas and metaphor, bridging theology, politics, and art in a single breath. Cleverness here is communal—belonging to the culture, not the individual. It is intellect with humility—rare, and therefore radical.

Across Asia, cleverness remains a serious business, measured differently depending on the culture. In Japan and Korea, intellect is measured by mastery; in China, by context; in India, by synthesis. The Japanese intellectual speaks softly, leaving space for reflection. The Chinese intellectual couches insight in parable. The Indian intellectual combines ancient philosophy with modern audacity—quoting the Bhagavad Gita and Silicon Valley in the same sentence. Asian intellect is not performative in volume but in precision. It seeks harmony, not applause—though applause inevitably follows.

Across Africa and Latin America, cleverness takes the form of storytelling. The wise person is the one who can make a crowd listen, who can transmit knowledge through narrative rather than declaration. In Lagos or Accra, intellect is rhythmic: thought carried in proverb, irony in laughter. In Mexico City or Buenos Aires, it is emotional: intellect mixed with memory, resistance, and rhythm. These are places where the cleverest voice is the one that makes others feel clever too—intellect as gift rather than display.

The Global Factory of Smarts

Modern platforms have industrialised the production of

intellectual display. Every LinkedIn user is a thought leader. Every podcaster is a philosopher. Every person with a Twitter account is a public intellectual. We have democratised expertise so thoroughly that expertise has become meaningless. Everyone is an expert on everything. The conspiracy of cleverness is now so complete that we have lost the ability to distinguish between actual knowledge and confident opinion.

The result is a world drowning in commentary where actual understanding has become invisible. The person who has spent ten years studying a subject is outpaced by the person who spent an afternoon reading about it and can tweet about it compellingly. The careful researcher is buried under the noise of confident assertions. The humble scholar is eclipsed by the charismatic charlatan.

The Cleverness Trap

The irony of the age of intellect is that we mistake complexity for depth. We talk about ideas the way we used to talk about possessions: mine, exclusive, valuable. But knowledge hoarded is knowledge lost. And cleverness without empathy is just ego with better vocabulary. The person who can explain quantum mechanics in a tweet is not necessarily smarter than the person who admits they do not understand it. But they are more likely to get followers.

We have created a system where the performance of thinking is rewarded more than actual thinking. Where the appearance of understanding is valued more than understanding itself. Where the ability to sound intelligent has become more important than being intelligent. And so everyone performs, everyone displays, everyone signals their cleverness—and nobody actually learns anything because we are all too busy proving how much we already know.

Cultural Cures for Performative Intellect

From America: keep the optimism, lose the sales pitch. Actually disagree sometimes. Show uncertainty occasionally.

From Britain: keep the irony, but let sincerity breathe. Your wit is elegant, but it can also obscure.

From France: keep the style, add humility. Beauty is wonderful, but so is truth.

From Germany: keep the rigour, add laughter. Precision is valuable, but so is play.

From Eastern Europe: keep the realism, rediscover joy. Cynicism is wise, but so is hope.

From Scandinavia: keep the modesty, risk passion. Restraint is admirable, but so is conviction.

From the Mediterranean: keep the fire, seek clarity. Emotion is honest, but so is directness.

From Asia: keep the discipline, share the wisdom. Control is wise, but so is vulnerability.

From Africa and Latin America: keep the story, let others tell theirs. Your narrative is valuable, but so are theirs.

Conclusion: Beyond Cleverness

True intelligence has never been about showing what we know. It is about what we do when we do not know. The smartest people in the room are not the ones speaking—they are the ones still curious. They ask, listen, and connect ideas rather than defend them. They are comfortable with ambiguity. They can hold multiple truths simultaneously. They do not need to prove their intelligence because their intelligence is expressed through what they do, not what they say.

In a world that worships cleverness, wisdom might just be the new rebellion. Because cleverness says, "Look at me. See how smart I am." Wisdom whispers, "Let us look together. Maybe we can understand this."

And that—across every culture, in every language, in every form of intelligence humanity possesses—is the rarest and most valuable thing of all.

CHAPTER EIGHTEEN: THE CULT OF CONFIDENCE

How Arrogance Became Aspirational

If the 20th century worshipped progress, the 21st worships confidence. Not wisdom, not kindness, not humility—just conviction, preferably delivered at volume. We live in an age where uncertainty is treated as a moral failing, where hesitation is considered weakness, and where humility has become an HR problem best solved by mandatory confidence training. The world does not ask, "Are you right?" It asks, "Are you sure?" And whoever answers loudest wins.

Confidence has become the currency of modern life. It is what gets you hired, elected, followed, believed. A confident person with no expertise will beat an expert plagued by doubt every single time. We have constructed societies where the person most certain of their rightness holds the most power, regardless of whether their certainty is warranted. The cult of confidence is perhaps the most pervasive religion of our age, and it is one with devastating consequences.

The Birth of Belief in the Self

Confidence once meant composure—knowing your place in a larger order, understanding your role, and fulfilling it with dignity. It was about equanimity in the face of uncertainty. Now it means creating that uncertainty by announcing your version of reality loudly enough that others begin to believe it. The self-help boom of the past fifty years taught us that success is ninety per cent mindset and ten per cent luck. The corollary, left unspoken but deeply felt, is that failure is ninety per cent lack of belief and ten per cent circumstance. We have been conditioned to believe that if we just believe hard enough, reality will conform to our beliefs.

The result is billions of people straining to manifest reality through posture and hashtags, through vision boards and affirmations, through the relentless performance of confidence. Somewhere between Nietzsche's Übermensch and Oprah's "You can do anything," humanity reinvented faith—in itself. We have replaced religious certainty with personal certainty, and the results are equally mixed.

America: Confidence as Manifest Destiny

The United States has industrialised confidence in ways that would astound previous generations. It is not merely admired; it is expected, demanded, rewarded. From Hollywood auditions to Silicon Valley pitch decks, from political campaigns to dating apps, certainty is moral currency. The American entrepreneur never says, "I think." They say, "I know." The American politician does not suggest; they declare. The American self-help guru does not propose; they promise. The American dream is built on the conviction that you can be anything you want to be if you believe it strongly enough.

The self-made myth runs deep in American culture. If you fail, you simply did not believe enough. Doubt is unpatriotic. Confidence is capitalism's camouflage. Yet it is also infectious. American optimism—loud, relentless, slightly delusional—remains the world's favourite export. Other nations complain about American arrogance, yet they secretly admire the confidence that allows Americans to attempt things that more cautious cultures would never dream of trying.

The American Cult of Confidence has produced genuine

innovation alongside genuine delusion. It has produced companies that changed the world and companies that were frauds from the start. It has produced leaders of vision and leaders of vanity. The problem is that the system rewards confidence regardless of outcomes. You can fail spectacularly in America and remain confident. You can fail again. And again. And eventually, if you maintain your confidence long enough, you might succeed—or you might simply become famous for your confidence itself.

Britain: Confidence with a Wink

The British, allergic to earnestness, practise a subtler faith in the self. Their confidence comes wrapped in irony and modesty. They call it "having a go," which really means: "I might fail, but I will make a joke about it before you can." True British confidence is the ability to seem self-deprecating whilst quietly convinced of one's superiority. Every nation fakes confidence; the British disguise it. They can dominate a room whilst appearing not to try. They can express absolute conviction whilst maintaining plausible deniability about doing so.

The cult of confidence in Britain is so well-disguised that foreigners often mistake British restraint for lack of confidence. The opposite is true. A Briton who shouts their confidence is insecure. A Briton who is quietly certain of their rightness whilst appearing amused by the entire situation is genuinely confident. The performance is so sophisticated that it has become almost invisible.

France: The Cult of Conviction

In France, confidence is a civic duty. The ability to speak with elegance and certainty—even when completely wrong—is a national right. The French intellectual does not doubt; they declare. The tone is lyrical, the logic occasionally optional, the confidence exquisite. It is arrogance reimagined as artistry. You do not have to be right—you just have to sound magnificent being wrong. The French Cult of Confidence assumes that style and substance are inseparable, that how you say something is as important as what you say, and that if you say it beautifully enough, the distinction between opinion and fact becomes meaningless.

Germany: The Competence Creed

German confidence rests on competence. No grandstanding, no slogans—just precision. The engineer, the bureaucrat, the politician—all radiate quiet assurance born of preparation and mastery. Confidence here is not performative; it is procedural. A German does not say, "Trust me." They say, "Here are the specifications." It is certainty through system—confidence earned, not improvised. The Cult of Confidence in Germany is actually a cult of correctness. You can be confident if, and only if, you have done the work to justify that confidence.

Eastern Europe: The Cynical Confidence

Eastern Europe does confidence differently: through irony and weary endurance. Centuries of history have bred scepticism too deep for self-delusion. The Polish businessman, the Czech intellectual, the Hungarian politician—all display a kind of weary conviction. It is not "I can do it," but "Someone has to, so it might as well be me." Their confidence is pragmatic, fatalistic, and strangely attractive. They have learned that arrogance is pointless, but endurance is power. You do not need to be confident that you will succeed; you just need to be confident that you will survive.

Scandinavia: The Quiet Certainty

In Scandinavia, confidence hides behind calm. Overt self-promotion violates social code; competence speaks for itself. The Swede does not shout; they demonstrate. The Dane does not boast; they deliver. The Norwegian simply hikes a mountain and smiles modestly from the summit. Here, the truly confident person is the one who never needs to prove it. The Cult of Confidence in Scandinavia is a conspiracy of restraint—the understanding that real confidence is so complete it requires no validation.

Italy and Spain: The Charismatic Gospel

In the Mediterranean, confidence is theatre. Volume, gesture, charm—all perfectly acceptable substitutes for evidence. The Italian does not "believe" in themselves; they perform belief until it becomes true. The Spanish mix pride with passion—confidence as emotion, not strategy. Failure is not shameful here; it is dramatic material. Confidence regenerates instantly with the next espresso, the next conversation, the next opportunity to perform belief again. The Cult of Confidence in Southern Europe is perhaps the most infectious because it is so thoroughly joyful.

The Middle East: Dignity as Strength

Across the Arab world, confidence is expressed through composure. Loudness is vulgar; calm is power. The leader, the scholar, the poet—each commands respect through gravity. Self-belief is inseparable from faith and honour. A confident man or woman here is not the one who speaks first, but the one whose silence others wait to break. The Cult of Confidence in the Middle East is quiet and deep, rooted in tradition and belief systems that predate modern psychology.

Asia: The Discipline of Belief

In Asia, confidence often hides beneath humility. It is quiet, methodical, collective—confidence without arrogance. In Japan and Korea, mastery is the measure. In China, achievement speaks louder than self-praise. In India, confidence is rhetorical: big dreams, bigger metaphors, and unshakeable optimism beneath the chaos. Asian confidence is not loud, but it is long-term—belief expressed through perseverance rather than performance.

Africa and Latin America: Confidence as Collective Energy

Across Africa and Latin America, confidence flows communally. It is rhythm, movement, presence—the sense that "we" can do anything. African confidence is grounded in pride of place; Latin confidence, in joy of performance. Both reject shame as unproductive and celebrate resilience as destiny. It is not self-help—it is self-celebration. The Cult of Confidence here is tribal: individual confidence matters less than collective belief in the group's capacity.

The Dark Side of Certainty

The Cult of Confidence rewards certainty over reflection. We hire charisma, elect bravado, and follow whoever sounds most convinced. The loud shape the world; the thoughtful are left to clean it up. Confidence has become the camouflage of the insecure—the louder we proclaim, the less we question. And humility, once the mark of wisdom, now risks being mistaken for weakness.

The problem with the Cult of Confidence is that it creates a world where the most dangerous people are the most certain. The confident fool is more dangerous than the hesitant wise person because the fool's certainty attracts followers. We have built systems that reward confidence regardless of competence, that elevate the certain regardless of correctness. The result is a world led by people who are very sure of things they should be uncertain about.

Cultural Remedies for the Confidence Crisis

From America: keep the optimism, rediscover doubt. Confidence matters, but certainty about complex problems is often arrogance.

From Britain: keep the humour, risk sincerity. Your irony is elegant, but sometimes things need to be said plainly.

From France: keep the elegance, accept imperfection. Perfection is the enemy of progress.

From Germany: keep the precision, soften the delivery. Correctness matters, but so does connection.

From Eastern Europe: keep the endurance, add hope. You have survived, and that is impressive, but so is believing things might improve.

From Scandinavia: keep the calm, allow pride. Confidence is not arrogance; it is the acknowledgement of competence.

From the Mediterranean: keep the passion, add reflection. Enthusiasm is contagious, but so is thought.

From Asia: keep the discipline, risk vulnerability. Restraint is wise, but so is admitting uncertainty.

From Africa and Latin America: keep the joy, add accountability. Collective confidence is powerful, but so is individual responsibility.

Conclusion: The Courage of Uncertainty

Real confidence is not the absence of doubt; it is the decision to continue despite it. The truly self-assured person can say, "I do not know," and still command respect. Because certainty dominates; curiosity inspires. And in a world where everyone is shouting their confidence, the person who can acknowledge their uncertainty is often the bravest of all.

The next evolution of confidence may not look like a pose at all. It may be the willingness to say "I do not know" and actually mean it. It may be the courage to change your mind. It may be the strength to admit error. Because the most confident people are often the ones least afraid of being wrong.

CHAPTER NINETEEN: FROM DIALOGUE TO DUEL

How Conversation Became a Blood Sport

There was a time when conversation was about discovery —a way to share, compare, and connect. Two minds meeting, each bringing their own experience and understanding, and through the act of speaking and listening, both leaving with something they did not have before. Now conversation is a duel. Every exchange has a winner and a loser. Every opinion must be defended to the death. And everyone, apparently, is armed with statistics, screenshots, and the certainty that they are right and everyone who disagrees is not just wrong but dangerous, stupid, or both.

We used to ask, "What do you think?" with genuine curiosity about the answer. Now we demand, "Whose side are you on?" as though there are only two sides and neutrality is betrayal. The stakes have been raised so high that a simple disagreement about policy feels like a personal attack. A different political opinion feels like a threat to civilisation itself. We have weaponised disagreement and turned the humble conversation into a battleground.

The Weaponisation of Words

Language, once a bridge between people, has become a battleground. Online, every sentence is a potential landmine.

Offline, every pause is a potential weakness. We duel not with swords but with statistics, sarcasm, and screenshots. The old rules of rhetoric—listen, consider, reply thoughtfully—have been replaced by new ones: interrupt, escalate, post immediately, screenshots for proof. Disagreement is no longer dialogue; it is performance. The audience is not your opponent; it is everyone watching, and your goal is to win them over, to make your opponent look foolish, to dominate the space.

We have turned conversation into a contact sport with rules designed to reward aggression and punish nuance. The person who can shout loudest wins. The person who can be most inflammatory gains followers. The person who can reduce a complex issue to an insult gets amplified. The algorithm has trained us to duel, and we have become very good at it.

America: The Theatre of Outrage

In the United States, argument has gone professional. The talk show, the debate stage, the comment section—all follow the same logic: conflict equals ratings, outrage equals engagement, and the person who can generate the most heat wins. The American Duelist thrives on momentum. They interrupt before you finish, summarise your point incorrectly, and then destroy their own version of it. It is not malice—it is choreography perfected over decades.

Each speaker rehearses the role of righteous victim. They collect evidence of their persecution. They frame every disagreement as an existential threat. They perform outrage with such conviction that you begin to believe the stakes really are as high as they claim. And when the shouting stops, the audience applauds. The rating goes up. Advertisers are happy. Everyone has won except, of course, actual understanding.

The American duel assumes that debate is entertainment, that disagreement is content, and that the goal is not truth but victory. The winner is not the one who was right, but the one who was most entertaining whilst being wrong.

Britain: The Duel of Wit

British duelling is subtler but equally lethal. Here, the blade is irony, the parry understatement. A sharp "Indeed" can draw more blood than an American rant. The goal is not to crush the opponent—that would be vulgar—but to humiliate them politely. This is the House of Commons method: verbal fencing in tailored suits, where the rules of engagement are more important than the actual outcome.

The key rule? Never appear angry. Rage is for amateurs; ridicule is for professionals. The Brit who can demolish an argument with a perfectly timed joke whilst maintaining composure has won. The one who loses their temper has already lost the debate. British duelling is sophisticated, which makes it more dangerous. Your opponent will smile whilst destroying you. You will not realise you have been beaten until you are already down.

France: The Intellectual Joust

In France, argument is a national art form—passionate, elegant, and eternal. Two French intellectuals can debate a comma for three hours and both leave victorious because the point was never to win but to perform the debate beautifully. The duel here is philosophical, not personal. Victory lies in flourish, not finality. The French debater wields rhetoric like a rapier—dazzling, dangerous, and entirely unnecessary to the point. But it is glorious to watch.

The French understand something that Anglo-Saxon duellists often miss: that the performance of argument is more important than its resolution. You do not have to convince your opponent; you just have to make the audience believe you are worth listening to. The duel continues because the point is not agreement but engagement. French debate is designed never to end because the moment it ends, the theatre stops.

Germany: The Procedural Battle

German argumentation resembles a courtroom. Facts, structure, and order dominate; emotion is considered sabotage. The duel begins with data and ends with consensus, though often after thirty PowerPoint slides and a meeting to discuss scheduling the next meeting. Raising your voice is seen as intellectual collapse. This is not combat but chess—and only one side brought a rulebook.

The German approach assumes that if you can just get the facts right and present them logically enough, the other person will have no choice but to agree. This is admirable but sometimes naive. It assumes all disagreement stems from misunderstanding, when sometimes it stems from genuinely different values. The German duelist wins on points; the American wins on entertainment; the Brit wins on style.

Eastern Europe: The Fatalistic Feud

In Poland, Hungary, or the Balkans, argument has a darker flavour—half tragedy, half comedy. Debate here is existential theatre: history is always the third participant. Eastern European duelists do not argue to win but to survive the absurdity of it all. A shrug often carries more meaning than a speech. The most devastating line? "Nothing will change." It is not cynicism—it is memory. These are people who have watched ideologies rise and fall, watched certainty prove false, watched victors become victims.

The Eastern European duel assumes that all positions are partially correct and partially delusional, that history will prove everyone wrong eventually, and that the point is not victory but endurance. You duel to stay sharp, to maintain your wits, to prove you have not yet been crushed by the weight of history. The winner is the one still standing at the end, still capable of irony, still capable of laughter.

Scandinavia: The Duel That Never Happens

In Scandinavia, conflict is treated like bad weather—acknowledged, endured, and avoided whenever possible. Debate exists, but it is calm, procedural, and painfully civilised. The duel here is internal. Swedes will disagree silently, then quietly implement their version anyway. No need for bloodshed when consensus can be weaponised more effectively. Nordic societies do not fight to win; they fight to agree. The duel that appears not to be happening is the deadliest one.

The Scandinavian approach to argument is so effective precisely because it is so invisible. By the time you realise you have lost, you have already agreed you lost. The decision has been made. The meeting is over. And you are not even sure how it happened.

The Mediterranean: The Duel of Passion

In Italy, Spain, and Greece, debate is opera. Voices rise, arms wave, tempers flare—and then everyone hugs. Mediterranean duels are about emotion, not ego. To shout is to care. To stay silent is to offend. Arguments are performance art: fury followed by forgiveness. It is verbal catharsis—cleansing rather than conquering. You leave the argument angrier than when you entered, but somehow more connected to the person you were arguing with. The duel was not about winning; it was about proving you care enough to fight.

The Middle East: Honour in Disagreement

Across the Arab world, argument still retains a code of honour. Tone and respect matter more than victory. The duel begins with poetry, ends with coffee. You can argue fiercely as long as you preserve dignity. To insult is to lose face; to persuade gracefully is to win eternity. Even conflict is courteous. The duel here is not about dominance but about maintaining relationships whilst disagreeing. The person who can argue most fiercely whilst treating their opponent with most respect has won.

Asia: The Duel of Indirection

Across Asia, open confrontation is discouraged. Harmony is prized, disagreement implied. The Japanese duel through silence; the Chinese through allegory; the Indian through storytelling. A "Yes" may mean "No." A pause may mean "I am disappointed." The battlefield is subtext. To Western ears, it sounds peaceful; to insiders, it is psychological warfare. The quietest duelists often win because their opponent never realises they have been bested until it is too late.

Digital Duelling

Online, the duel has lost all rules. No tone, no pause, no empathy. Just infinite ammunition and no referee. The internet rewards outrage with visibility. Silence is now suspicious. Every thread becomes a miniature war zone where facts die first, nuance is buried under slogans, and the person with the most followers wins regardless of who was right. The duel has gone global—fought in comments, waged in memes, settled by algorithms that reward conflict.

Why We Fight

We duel because we fear being unseen. To agree feels invisible; to concede feels erased. So we attack, defend, posture—anything to stay audible. It is not hatred that drives us, but insecurity. Every argument is a plea: Listen to me. Take me seriously. Acknowledge that I exist and that my thoughts matter. The duel has become the way we prove we are alive.

We have forgotten that disagreement does not have to be a duel. That we can hold different opinions without it meaning we are enemies. That we can lose an argument without losing ourselves. We have turned every conversation into a battle because we have been taught that there are only two positions: winner or loser. There is no middle ground. There is no way to disagree and remain connected.

Cultural Remedies for the Verbal Arms Race

From America: Keep passion, lose performance. Actually listen to your opponent occasionally.

From Britain: Keep wit, add warmth. Your irony is elegant, but it can also create distance.

From France: Keep eloquence, seek empathy. Beauty is wonderful, but so is understanding.

From Germany: Keep order, allow emotion. Logic matters, but so does connection.

From Eastern Europe: Keep realism, rediscover hope. Cynicism is wise, but so is possibility.

From Scandinavia: Keep civility, risk disagreement. Consensus should not mean conformity.

From the Mediterranean: Keep fire, reduce volume. Passion is honest, but so is listening.

From Asia: Keep subtlety, risk honesty. Indirect communication works, but so does directness.

From Africa and Latin America: Keep rhythm, seek resolution. Your music is beautiful, but so is peace.

Conclusion: The Return of Dialogue

Dialogue, at its best, is not about victory; it is about discovery. It is not two voices shouting—it is two minds meeting halfway. But meeting halfway requires risk: the courage to be changed. It requires the willingness to admit you might be wrong. It requires the strength to listen more than you speak.

When we stop fighting to win and start listening to learn, the duel becomes what it was meant to be all along—not war, but wonder. Not combat, but connection. And suddenly, the possibility of actual understanding emerges from beneath the rubble of false certainty.

Because the most revolutionary sound in the modern world

might not be the last word, but the one that follows it—silence. The pause where listening can finally happen.

CHAPTER TWENTY: RECLAIMING THE PAUSE

How Stillness Became the New Subversion

fter years of relentless noise, the world feels tired. Every sentence online ends with urgency—"must read," "breaking," "now."

We are surrounded by people desperate to speak and terrified to stop. The pause has become extinct in our civilisation, replaced by the constant hum of voices competing for attention. And yet, beneath the din, something whispers: maybe civilisation does not end in silence. Maybe it begins there. To pause is to reclaim humanity. To pause is to say: I trust that my words will still be there when I am ready to speak them. To pause is to acknowledge that thinking matters more than reacting.

The Lost Rhythm of Conversation

A good conversation once had rhythm—question, reflection, response. Breath. Thought. Reply. The pause was where understanding happened, where meaning settled, where the next thought could be properly formed. Now it is all chorus, no verse. We speak faster, type faster, react faster—mistaking speed for intelligence. The pause, once the sacred space where thought lived, has been written out of the script entirely. Without rhythm, speech becomes static; without silence, meaning evaporates into the air like steam.

We are, quite literally, talking ourselves into incoherence. The more we speak, the less we say. The faster we communicate, the less we understand. We have optimised for velocity and lost everything else. We have built systems that reward the immediate response over the considered one, the snap judgment over the careful analysis, the first thought over the best thought. And in doing so, we have made real conversation nearly impossible.

Scandinavia: The Calm Blueprint

The Nordics remain the global custodians of pause. In Sweden, silence in meetings is not awkward; it is productive. Decisions made in silence tend to be better than decisions made in haste. In Denmark, pauses signal respect. To allow someone time to think before responding is to honour their thought. In Norway, silence is as natural as snowfall. People are comfortable with it. They do not fear it. A Swede once told me, "If no one speaks, it means everyone is thinking." It is not emptiness—it is trust. It is the understanding that real thought requires silence, and that good decisions come from thought, not from immediate reaction.

In a world that confuses noise with progress, the Scandinavian pause is quiet rebellion. It says: I trust that slowing down will lead somewhere better. I trust that thinking takes time. I trust that silence is not failure. Nordic boardrooms are temples of thoughtfulness, and it shows in the quality of decisions made there. The pause has not been eliminated; it has been protected, cultivated, and valued.

Japan: The Sacred Interval

In Japan, silence is art—the concept of ma, the space between things. It is not emptiness but fullness. A pause in Japanese conversation is not dead air; it is charged with meaning and attention. The Japanese listener's response—an aizuchi, a small sound or nod—signals presence without interruption. It communicates: I hear you completely. Now allow me to think about what you have said. This respect for space is woven into architecture, ceremony, and speech. It is civilisation built on rhythm rather than rush.

A Japanese conversation feels like music because it has pauses. The spaces between words are as important as the words themselves. A Western businessperson entering a Japanese meeting will often experience profound discomfort. Nobody is speaking. But everyone is listening, thinking, processing. Then, after a silence that feels like it lasts forever but is probably only thirty seconds, someone speaks. And what they say carries weight because it has been thought through in the silence that preceded it.

France: The Dramatic Pause

Even the French, who treat conversation as sport, understand the power of pause. In rhetoric, silence is not weakness; it is punctuation. The right hesitation—the lifted eyebrow, the hand in mid-air—gives the next phrase authority. The French pause is theatrical, precise, and intentional. It says, "I control the tempo." It says, "You will wait for my words because what I am about to say is worth waiting for." While others fear silence, the French manipulate it, use it, weaponise it. It is style as sovereignty.

Britain: The Awkward Pause

The British pause is famous—long, hesitant, slightly damp with embarrassment. It is a national reflex against saying too much. Entire friendships have been sustained on polite silence and the sound of tea being poured. Awkwardness is the price of restraint. But beneath the hesitations lies a form of civility—a refusal to fill air with nonsense. A well-timed pause in Britain can signal irritation, intimacy, or absolute contempt. It is conversational Morse code for the emotionally fluent. The British have perfected the art of saying nothing whilst saying everything through the strategic deployment of silence.

Eastern Europe: The Heavy Pause

In Poland, Hungary, and the Czech Republic, silence carries history. It is not meditative but wary—the residue of times when words could wound or condemn. Eastern Europeans pause not from politeness but from realism. A gap between sentences is a moment to measure risk. It is not comfortable silence—it is courageous. The stillness after truth, or before it. The pause that says: I have learned to think before I speak because my words have consequences. Eastern European silence is not weakness; it is the wisdom of survival.

The Middle East: The Honourable Pause

In the Arab world, the pause remains a gesture of dignity. To interrupt is to disrespect; to pause is to honour. Conversation flows like the rhythm of breath and poetry. Every silence carries hospitality—space for the other to exist, time for thought to settle. Even heated debate maintains structure: passion within boundaries. The pause is not absence but architecture. It is how a conversation is built so that everyone can stand safely within it.

The Mediterranean: The Impossible Pause

In Italy, Spain, and Greece, pauses are theoretical. To stop speaking would be unthinkable. Yet even here, silence appears—fleeting, dramatic, sacred. At the end of a rant, after laughter, before the next espresso—a pause arrives, shared, glowing with humanity. It lasts three seconds, maybe four, before someone interrupts it with, "Anyway..." But for those few seconds, it feels divine. The Mediterranean has learned that even in a world of constant talk, the pause has power precisely because it is so rare.

Asia: The Meditative Pause

Across Asia, the pause is wisdom embodied. In India, it lives in conversation as reflection before advice. In China, it signifies consideration—the stillness before strategy. In Korea, it shows respect: thoughtfulness as social currency. The Asian pause is discipline—language's inhale. It is how complexity becomes clarity. It is how someone demonstrates that they take your words seriously enough to think before replying. The pause here is not empty; it is full of processing, of consideration, of respect.

Africa: The Rhythmic Pause

Across Africa, conversation flows like music—speech, response, silence, drumbeat. The pause is pulse. It allows laughter to land, lets proverbs resonate, gives stories room to breathe. In the storytelling circles of Ghana or Kenya, silence means anticipation, not discomfort. The listener's hush is half the performance. The pause here is communal—meaning made in rhythm, not volume. The pause and the speech are partners, each giving the other meaning. Without silence, the story collapses. Without the story, the silence is just emptiness.

The Digital Deafness

Modern technology has rewired the human ear in ways we are only beginning to understand. We listen to sound, not speech. Podcasts, audiobooks, background chatter—we consume voices without connection. The "listener" today is multitasking, distracted, transactional. The screen talks; we pretend to hear. Every "heard" notification is a technological lie. We hear everything, but we listen to nothing. We have optimised for constant input and eliminated all pauses.

The pause is what algorithms cannot commodify. It cannot be monetised, packaged, or sold. It does not generate data. It does not create engagement metrics. So the algorithm actively punishes it. Every notification is designed to interrupt the pause. Every alert is calibrated to prevent silence. We have built technology specifically designed to eliminate the very thing that makes thought possible.

Why Listening Feels So Difficult

Listening requires the pause. Thinking requires the pause. Understanding requires the pause. Growth requires the pause. Yet we have built a world that punishes all of these things. We reward the quick response over the considered one. We celebrate the person who can think on their feet, not the person who can think deeply. We value the snap judgment over the careful analysis. We have made pauses into failures and mistakes into opportunities to move faster.

The pause is difficult because it requires surrender. It means admitting that you do not have an immediate answer. It means being comfortable with not knowing. It means trusting that meaning will emerge if you give it space. But in a culture addicted to its own certainty, this is terrifying. So we fill the pause with noise, any noise, something to prove we are still thinking, still processing, still present. But we are not. We are just performing presence whilst actually fleeing into distraction.

Cultural Remedies for the Vanishing Pause

From Japan: Embrace ma—the beauty of interval. The space between things contains meaning.

From Scandinavia: Trust silence to carry meaning. Create it deliberately and defend it fiercely.

From Eastern Europe: Let stillness express strength. Silence is not weakness; it is wisdom.

From the Middle East: Use pauses to honour presence. Silence is a form of respect made audible.

From Africa: Feel rhythm between words. Silence is part of the music, not a break in it.

From Britain: Turn awkwardness into art. The pause can be powerful if you let it.

From France: Control tempo, not volume. Strategic silence

amplifies what comes after.

From the Mediterranean: Let emotion rest before it rises again. The pause allows the heart to catch up with the voice.

From the Americas: Rediscover quiet without guilt. Stillness is not failure; it is thinking.

Silence as Resistance

To pause in today's world is to rebel. To wait before responding, to think before posting, to listen without rushing to reply—these are acts of cultural courage. Every civilisation that forgot how to pause eventually forgot how to think. The pause is not retreat. It is return. It is the reclamation of our capacity to actually process information rather than merely react to it.

The person who can sit with silence, who can allow a conversation to breathe, who can resist the urge to fill every gap with noise—that person is practicing radical self-care. They are protecting their own thinking. They are defending their own capacity for understanding. They are saying: I matter enough to think carefully about what I say.

Conclusion: The Quiet Renaissance

To reclaim the pause is to reclaim ourselves. It is to say that we are not merely vessels for information transfer, responding as quickly as possible to every stimulus. It is to assert that thinking matters, that reflection has value, that understanding is worth the time it takes. It is to remember that we are human beings, not processing machines.

The pause is not extinct—merely endangered. It survives in churches, forests, libraries, and occasionally in conversation between people who trust each other enough not to fill the air needlessly. It waits in the spaces between screens, in the moments before the next notification arrives. It persists in cultures that have not yet fully surrendered to the noise economy.

If the next great revolution in communication is not a new platform but a pause—a deliberate slowdown, a conscious choice to think before speaking, a commitment to listening without immediately planning a response—then perhaps we have a chance. Perhaps we can rebuild conversation as something other than a competition. Perhaps we can remember what it means to actually hear one another.

Because in the end, the most eloquent line in any conversation might still be the one no one utters. The pause where understanding happens. The silence where meaning lives. The space where, if we are very quiet, very still, and very brave, we might actually hear one another at last.

CHAPTER TWENTY-ONE: BACK TO US

*How We Begin Talking
Like Humans Again*

It started with noise. A world of voices shouting to be heard, competing for attention, mistaking volume for value. We spoke louder, faster, more often. We interrupted before others could finish. We performed instead of connecting. We broadcast instead of conversed. And somewhere in the cacophony, we lost something essential. We lost each other. Now, as the talking tide begins to ebb—as people everywhere feel the exhaustion of endless noise, as platforms begin to fail under the weight of their own toxicity, as communities fracture from too much shouting—we stand on quieter ground. Perhaps what we have been seeking all along is not to be heard, but to belong.

If the 2010s and 2020s were the decades of "Back to Me," then perhaps the 2030s and beyond could yet be "Back to Us." Not through legislation or technology, but through the slow, deliberate choice of individuals to listen instead of shout, to connect instead of perform, to value understanding over victory. It will not happen automatically. It will require intention. It will require courage. It will require us to swim against the current of every algorithm, every incentive structure, every cultural message that tells us to prioritise ourselves. But it is possible. And if enough of us choose it, perhaps it can become inevitable.

The End of the Monologue Era

Every civilisation produces its own particular madness. Ours chose self-expression. We spent decades learning to speak, to post, to pitch, and to perform. We mastered every tone except tenderness. We became fluent in persuasion and illiterate in presence. The louder the world grew, the lonelier it felt. We filled our lives with followers but emptied them of friends. We collected validation but lost meaning. We were heard everywhere and understood nowhere.

The Monologue Era is dying. Not because we have run out of things to say—we will never do that. But because we have finally begun to notice that saying things does not make us happy. Being heard does not make us feel less alone. Winning arguments does not make us feel more connected. We are beginning, slowly and painfully, to understand that the problem was never that we were not being listened to. The problem was that we were not listening.

The Return of the Listener

The hero of the future will not be the speaker, but the listener. The person who can sit through disagreement without flinching, who can absorb complexity without reducing it into slogans, who can resist the urge to dominate and instead invite. Listening is the new radicalism. In a culture addicted to amplification, attention is an act of generosity. Every time we choose to hear rather than reply, we rebuild the bridge that ego burned.

This will not be easy. We have trained ourselves out of listening. We have built brains that are optimised for distraction and reaction. Our bodies are flooded with cortisol every time we feel unheard. Our social media feeds punish silence and reward noise. Everything in our environment conspires to keep us talking. Yet listening is still possible. It is still there, waiting in the quiet moments, in the spaces between notifications, in the conversations where people still believe in the value of understanding over victory.

The Rediscovery of Dialogue

Dialogue is not compromise; it is choreography. It is the movement of meaning between people who care more about truth than triumph. It is the willingness to be changed by another person's words. It is the understanding that your view might be incomplete, that the other person might have insight you lack, that disagreement can be an opportunity rather than a threat.

Across the world, from Japanese tea houses to Ghanaian storytelling circles, from Scandinavian boardrooms to Mediterranean dinner tables, dialogue is still sacred in pockets. It is not just words exchanged—it is recognition offered. It is the oldest peace treaty on earth: two people agreeing that understanding matters more than victory. If we could rebuild this globally, if we could make dialogue the default rather than the exception, we might actually change something fundamental about how we live together.

The Cultural Tapestry of Togetherness

Each culture has something essential to teach about how to come back to us. These lessons have always been there; we simply stopped listening:

From America: rediscover optimism that includes others. Your belief in possibility is beautiful; now extend it to include that others might be right about things.

From Britain: pair humour with humility. Your wit is elegant; now add the courage to be sincere occasionally.

From France: balance conviction with grace. Your eloquence is magnificent; now use it to illuminate rather than dominate.

From Germany: use reason to serve compassion. Your logic is valuable; now let it inform empathy, not replace it.

From Eastern Europe: remember endurance without cynicism.

You have survived; now believe that others deserve to thrive, not just survive.

From Scandinavia: let calm lead. Your restraint is wise; now risk being passionate about connection.

From the Mediterranean: keep passion, share space. Your warmth is infectious; now make sure everyone gets a turn to speak.

From the Middle East: speak with dignity, listen with honour. Your grace is timeless; now extend it to those who disagree with you.

From Asia: find harmony between self and society. Your discipline is admirable; now use it to build bridges, not walls.

From Africa and Latin America: make joy communal, not competitive. Your music is beautiful; now let it unite rather than divide.

If we could listen to the world the way the world listens to itself —if we could hear all these voices together, not as competition but as chorus—we might finally understand what civilisation sounds like when it is kind.

The Age of the Conversational Citizen

In the next era, power will belong not to those who dominate, but to those who connect. The conversational citizen will not ask, "Who is right?" but "What is missing?" They will move easily between cultures, understanding that speech without context is just noise in translation. They will understand that real progress depends on empathy—and that empathy depends on silence long enough to hear.

These people are already among us. They are the teachers who ask genuine questions and wait for real answers. They are the parents who listen to their children without immediately offering solutions. They are the friends who can disagree without disconnecting. They are the leaders who admit when they are wrong. They are quiet in a loud world, which makes them remarkable. They are the future, if we choose to follow them.

The New Literacy

We have spent the last century teaching reading, writing, and rhetoric. We have built institutions around these skills. We have measured intelligence by the ability to read quickly, write clearly, and speak persuasively. Now we must teach something we have almost forgotten: listening, pausing, and reflecting. Conversation is civilisation's quiet software—and we have been running it on ego. To upgrade, we need only one update: replace "I" with "we."

It is astonishing how often the solution hides in the syntax. The problems we face as global societies are not fundamentally problems of communication; they are problems of connection. We know how to build weapons, but we have forgotten how to build bridges. We know how to win arguments, but we have forgotten how to resolve conflicts. We know how to broadcast, but we have forgotten how to dialogue. The solution is not more technology. It is more humanity.

The Courage to Be Small

Coming "back to us" does not mean erasing the self; it means resizing it. We can still be brilliant, loud, funny, ambitious —but not at the expense of coherence. Humility is not self-erasure; it is emotional architecture. It allows us to stand tall without standing on anyone. Perhaps the future leader, teacher, or influencer will not be the one who commands the room, but the one who makes others want to speak in it. The person whose power is expressed not through domination but through creating space.

This is harder than it sounds. We have been trained to believe that our worth is measured by how much we are heard, how many followers we have, how often our name appears. To voluntarily step back, to make space for others, to prioritise understanding over recognition—this feels like losing. But it is actually winning. It is winning at the only game worth playing: the game of building a world where people actually know and understand each other.

The Global Pause

Imagine a world where conversations slowed to human speed again—where the pause before speaking was not fear, but care. Where arguments ended not in triumph, but in understanding. Where silence meant thinking, not defeat. Where being quiet was not a liability but a strength. Where the person who listened most was respected most. Imagine a culture of conversation that spanned continents, where British irony existed alongside American warmth, where French eloquence existed beside Japanese stillness, where Nigerian rhythm existed beside Nordic calm.

That world exists already. We just talk too loudly to hear it. We are all standing in the same room, all capable of genuine connection, all hungry to be understood. But we are so busy broadcasting that we cannot hear anyone else broadcasting. We are so certain we are right that we cannot hear anyone saying something different. We are so desperate to be seen that we cannot see anyone else.

The Quiet Revolution

It begins, as revolutions always do, with one sentence: "Tell me what you think."

Then, the harder part: we wait. We actually wait. We do not interrupt. We do not plan our response. We do not scroll through our phones. We do not think about what we will say next. We just listen. We hear what the other person is actually saying, not what we think they are saying. We notice the emotion beneath the words. We understand the fear or hope or longing that prompted them to speak. We acknowledge that they exist, that their thoughts matter, that they deserve to be heard.

This simple act—genuine listening—is revolutionary in a world that has forgotten how to do it. It is an act of radical respect. It is a rejection of the entire system that says your worth is measured by how loudly you can speak. It is an assertion that understanding matters more than victory. It is a bet that connection is possible if we are brave enough to attempt it.

And it starts with pause. With silence. With the courage to stop speaking and start listening.

Conclusion: The Sound of Understanding

We have spent this entire book exploring how we talk past each other, how we dominate conversations, how we perform rather than connect. We have examined the ways that different cultures approach the fundamental human act of speaking and listening. We have looked at what happens when we mistake volume for value, performance for connection, being heard for being understood.

Now we come to the end, and the question is: what do we do with this knowledge?

The answer is simple but not easy: we begin again. We begin to listen. We begin to pause. We begin to believe that understanding is possible. We begin to trust that the person we disagree with is not an enemy but a human being with their own fears and hopes and reasons for believing what they believe.

We do this not because it will be easy. It will not be. We will slip back into old patterns. We will interrupt. We will perform. We will prioritise being heard over understanding. We will make mistakes. We will fail. But we will try. And every time we try —every time we choose to listen instead of speak, to pause instead of interrupt, to ask instead of declare—we build back the capacity for real conversation.

And real conversation, across all cultures, in all languages, in all forms of human connection, is still the only thing that has ever truly changed the world.

Because at the end of all the noise, after all the arguments and broadcasts and performances, after all the certainty and the duelling and the performance of confidence, there is only one thing that matters: whether we actually understand each other. Whether we have heard what someone is really saying. Whether we have allowed ourselves to be changed by another person's truth.

That is not "Back to Me."

That is "Back to Us."

And it is where we must go.

QUENTIN DRUMMOND ANDERSON

EPILOGUE: THE LUNCH THAT STARTED IT ALL

Boodles, St James's—A Quiet Afternoon of Noise

Every book has an origin story. This one began, fittingly, in conversation. Four old friends—veterans of life, laughter, and too many opinions—gathered for lunch at Boodles, the venerable St James's club where time seems to slow politely between courses. We had known each other since our teens or early twenties—school, mischief, travel, the decades-long dialogue of friendship. There were prawns, then grouse or the delicious mixed grill, then talk. The conversation, as always, began well-mannered and soon became gloriously chaotic: politics, books, wives and girlfriends, the usual theatre of men who have known one another too long to pretend to listen.

Christoph said, in exasperation, "For God's sake, it is always back to me with you lot."

And there it was. Three words that distilled an entire civilisation. The table fell into that rarest of things in Boodles: silence. Then laughter. Then the beginnings of a book. What started as a quip over claret became a question—and then a journey: Why do we all talk so much, so loudly, and so badly? What happened to listening, to nuance, to the joy of actual dialogue?

By pudding, we had outlined the whole idea. By port, we were arguing about the title. By coffee, no one was listening again. It was perfect. It was exactly the problem we were trying to describe.

And yours truly then and there decided it was his next project, and the ball started rolling. A number of months later..voila..I hope the three, at the very least might enjoy it!

Acknowledgements

To my fellow conspirators of conversation that day—R, C, and M—thank you for your wit, warmth, and the kind of friendship that can survive disagreement, digression, and dessert-pudding ! Without you, this book would have remained what most good conversations are meant to be: forgotten but somehow formative.

To the many people across continents who talked, listened, interrupted, and occasionally paused: thank you for teaching me that the world still hums with humanity when we stop trying to win it. Your stories, your perspectives, your ways of speaking and listening have shaped these pages.

To those who believed that a book about conversation mattered: thank you for your faith that in an age of noise, silence still has value.

And to the readers: may this book remind you that every story, every culture, and every voice deserves its turn. And when the turn is over—a pause. A moment of silence. A chance for someone else to speak.

BACK TO ME: THE GLOBAL ART OF TALKING WITHOUT LISTENING

ABOUT THE AUTHOR: QUENTIN DRUMMOND ANDERSON

Quentin Drummond Anderson is a writer, historian, and entrepreneur whose career has taken him from the boardrooms of global brands to the battlefields of history—and, occasionally, back to the lunch tables of St James's. Educated in Britain and seasoned by travel across four continents, Anderson has spent a lifetime listening to—and occasionally surviving—some of the world's most fascinating and deadly conversations.

As Executive Chairman of DVC Consultants and co-founder of ventures spanning fintech, social media, and AI-driven innovation, Anderson brings a strategist's precision and a storyteller's wit to every subject he tackles. His twenty published books and fifteen audiobooks range from military history and leadership to culture, innovation, and now, the psychology of human communication.

His acclaimed *Væringjar Trilogy* explores the intrigue of the Byzantine world, while *The Norman Chronicles Trilogy* traces the rise of the Norman warriors who reshaped Europe. In *The Duke's Shadow*, he masterfully intertwines politics and power in medieval England. His non-fiction works, including *Righteous Renegades: Once Hidden Heroes of the Holocaust* and *The Few Against the Many*, reveal his deep fascination with courage under pressure—whether on the battlefield or in the corridors of diplomacy. *The Fearless Fifteen: How the SAS Changed the Face of War* further cements his reputation for turning rigorous research into gripping human stories.

His three Short Story Collections : *Tales From The Tail,Tales From The Village and Short Stories from Tech* all expose the frailties of mankind in different scenarios.

With *Back to Me: The Global Art of Talking Without Listening*, Anderson turns his sharp eye for leadership and conflict toward a different kind of battleground—the modern conversation. Drawing on decades of observation from boardrooms, book launches, and Boodles lunches alike, he examines the cultural comedy and quiet tragedy of a world that talks too much and listens too little.

When not writing or advising on brand orchestration and technology disruption, Anderson divides his time between London and the quieter corners of the countryside—though those who know him suspect he is never truly off duty. You can find him, appropriately, still in conversation—online, in print, and occasionally in person, reminding his friends, with a wry smile, to take turns speaking.

SOURCES AND ACKNOWLEDGEMENTS

SOURCES AND FURTHER READING

FOUNDATIONAL TEXTS ON CONVERSATION AND COMMUNICATION

Goffman, Erving. The Presentation of Self in Everyday Life. Doubleday, 1959.

The seminal text on how we perform identity in social contexts. Essential for understanding conversation as performance rather than mere information exchange. Goffman's concept of "impression management" underpins much of the book's analysis of how we present ourselves in conversation.

Tannen, Deborah. You Just Don't Understand: Women and Men in Conversation. William Morrow, 1990.

Foundational work on gendered communication patterns. Tannen's distinction between "report talk" and "rapport talk" informs the analysis of how gender shapes conversational style across cultures.

Sacks, Harvey. Lectures on Conversation. Blackwell, 1992.

The founding text of conversation analysis. Sacks' work on turn-taking, repair mechanisms, and sequential organisation of talk provides the theoretical framework for understanding how conversation is actually structured.

Brown, Penelope and Stephen Levinson. Politeness: Some Universals in Language Usage. Cambridge University Press, 1987.

Essential for understanding how different cultures balance face-saving with directness. Their "positive face" and "negative face" framework informs the analysis of politeness across cultures.

Lakoff, Robin. The Language War. University of California Press, 2000.

Explores how language reflects and shapes power dynamics. Particularly valuable for understanding how gender, class, and cultural position shape who gets to speak and how.

CULTURAL PSYCHOLOGY AND CROSS-CULTURAL COMMUNICATION

Hofstede, Geert. Cultures and Organisations: Software of the Mind. McGraw-Hill, 2010.

Hofstede's cultural dimensions (individualism/collectivism, power distance, uncertainty avoidance, etc.) provide framework for understanding why different cultures approach communication so differently. His research on 50+ countries informs the book's comparative analysis.

Nisbett, Richard E. The Geography of Thought: How Asians and Westerners Think Differently... and Why. Free Press, 2003.

Explains fundamental differences in how Eastern and Western minds process information, relationships, and contradiction. Essential for understanding why, for example, Japanese listeners are comfortable with silence whilst American listeners find it threatening.

Hall, Edward T. The Silent Language. Doubleday, 1959.

Hall's distinction between "high-context" and "low-context" communication is foundational to the book's analysis of how different cultures encode meaning differently. His work explains why British irony works so differently from American directness.

Trompenaars, Fons and Charles Hampden-Turner. Riding the Waves of Culture: Understanding Diversity in Global Business. Nicholas Brealey Publishing, 1997.

Builds on Hofstede's framework with additional cultural dimensions relevant to communication style. Particularly useful for understanding variation within Western Europe.

Spencer-Oatey, Helen (ed.). Culturally Speaking: Culture, Communication and Politeness Theory. Continuum, 2000.

Collection of essays on how politeness is expressed differently across cultures. Directly informs the analysis of British understatement vs. American enthusiasm vs. Mediterranean warmth.

NEUROSCIENCE AND TRIBAL PSYCHOLOGY

Lieberman, Matthew D. Social: Why Our Brains Are Wired to Connect. Crown, 2013.

Explains the neurobiology of belonging, social pain, and the reward systems that keep us in groups. Essential for understanding why tribal belonging is so neurologically powerful that it shapes perception.

Sapolsky, Robert M. Behave: The Biology of Humans at Our Best and Worst. Penguin Press, 2017.

Comprehensive examination of the neural and hormonal systems underlying human behaviour, including tribalism, empathy, and conflict. Particularly relevant for understanding attribution bias and in-group/out-group psychology.

Damasio, Antonio. Descartes' Error: Emotion, Reason, and the Human Brain. Putnam, 1994.

Foundational neuroscience text explaining how emotion and reason are inseparable. Informs understanding of why pure logic cannot overcome tribal belonging—emotion is embedded in decision-making at neurological level.

Kandel, Eric R. In Search of Memory: The Emergence of a New Science of Mind. W.W. Norton, 2006.

While broader than just tribalism, Kandel's work on memory and learning explains how tribal patterns become embedded in neural pathways. Once learnt, they become automatic.

QUENTIN DRUMMOND ANDERSON

SOCIAL PSYCHOLOGY AND GROUP BEHAVIOUR

Tajfel, Henri and John C. Turner. "An Integrative Theory of Intergroup Conflict." The Social Psychology of Intergroup Relations, edited by W.G. Austin and S. Worchel, Brooks/Cole, 1979.

Social Identity Theory explains why people identify with groups and discriminate against out-groups even when group membership is arbitrary. Fundamental to understanding how tribes maintain cohesion through exclusion.

Sherif, Muzafer, et al. The Robbers Cave Experiment: Intergroup Conflict and Cooperation. University of Oklahoma Press, 1961.

Classic experimental demonstration that competition for resources increases intergroup hostility, while superordinate goals (shared objectives) reduce it. Informs discussion of how tribal conflict is created and resolved.

Moscovici, Serge. Social Influence and Social Change. Academic Press, 1976.

Explains how minorities within groups can shift group consensus through persistent, consistent alternative viewpoints. Relevant to understanding how tribal opinion is formed and can be changed.

Cialdini, Robert. Influence: The Psychology of Persuasion. Harper Business, 2006.

Examines the psychological principles of persuasion, including social proof and authority. Explains why people default to group opinion rather than independent judgment.

LANGUAGE, RHETORIC, AND POLITICAL SPEECH

Aristotle. Rhetoric. Translated by W. Rhys Roberts, Dover, 2004.

The foundational text on persuasion and the art of speaking. Aristotle's understanding that rhetoric is fundamentally about adaptation to audience remains the best framework for understanding how speakers tailor their message.

Burke, Kenneth. A Grammar of Motives. University of California Press, 1945.

Burke's "pentad" (act, scene, agent, agency, purpose) provides a framework for understanding how narratives are constructed and meaning is negotiated through language.

Perelman, Chaïm and Lucie Olbrechts-Tyteca. The New Rhetoric: A Treatise on Argumentation. University of Notre Dame Press, 1969.

Explains that argumentation is fundamentally about addressing audiences with shared values. Informs understanding of why tribal arguments are so effective (shared values) and cross-tribal arguments so difficult (conflicting values).

Lakoff, George. Moral Politics: How Liberals and Conservatives Think. University of Chicago Press, 2002.

Explains that political disagreement is fundamentally about different moral frameworks ("strict father" vs. "nurturant parent" models). Shows why rational argument cannot bridge tribal divides when underlying frameworks differ.

Sunstein, Cass R. Going to Extremes: How Like Minds Unite and Divide. Oxford University Press, 2009.

Explains "group polarisation" effect: when like-minded people deliberate together, they tend to adopt more extreme versions of their initial views. Foundational for understanding how tribes become more certain and less flexible over time.

DIGITAL COMMUNICATION AND SOCIAL MEDIA

boyd, danah. It's Complicated: The Social Lives of Networked Teens. Yale University Press, 2014.

While focused on teenagers, boyd's analysis of how social media shapes identity performance and tribal belonging applies across age groups. Essential for understanding digital tribalism.

Turkle, Sherry. Alone Together: Why We Expect More from Technology and Less from Each Other. Basic Books, 2011.

Explores how technology creates the illusion of connection whilst eroding actual connection. Directly addresses why digital platforms reward performance over presence.

Pariser, Eli. The Filter Bubble: What the Internet Is Hiding from You. Penguin Press, 2011.

Essential text on algorithmic curation and its role in creating ideological echo chambers. Directly informs Chapter 12 analysis of feedback loops.

Williams, James. Stand Out of Our Light: Freedom and Resistance in the Attention Economy. Cambridge University Press, 2018.

Examines how technology companies capture attention and reshape human agency. Explains structural reasons why digital listening has become nearly impossible.

Zuboff, Shoshana. The Age of Surveillance Capitalism: The Fight for a Human Future at the New Frontier of Power. PublicAffairs, 2019.

Comprehensive examination of how social media platforms extract data and use it to shape behaviour. Provides economic and technological explanation for why platforms reward outrage and punish nuance.

Haidt, Jonathan. The Righteous Mind: Why Good People Are Divided by Politics and Religion. Pantheon Books, 2012.

Explains the psychological basis of moral tribalism and why people with different moral foundations talk past each other. Essential for understanding ideological tribes and why cross-tribal conversation is so difficult.

LISTENING AND SILENCE

Nichols, Michael P. The Lost Art of Listening: How Learning to Listen Can Improve Relationships. Guilford Press, 1995.

One of the few books specifically about listening. Distinguishes between hearing and listening, and explains the psychological barriers to genuine listening.

Ong, Walter J. Orality and Literacy: The Technologizing of the Word. Routledge, 1982.

Historical analysis of how writing and printing changed how we think and listen. Provides context for why modern communication privileges speed over depth.

Cage, John. 4'33". Edition Peters, 1960.

Whilst technically a musical composition, Cage's silent piece raises essential questions about what silence means and what happens in the spaces between sound. Relevant to the philosophical dimension of the book's argument about pauses.

CULTURAL ANALYSIS AND SPECIFIC CULTURES

Paxman, Jeremy. The English: A Portrait of a People. Michael Joseph, 1998.

Excellent analysis of English communication style, including the role of irony, understatement, and what is left unspoken. Informs analysis of British conversation patterns.

Cohen, Roger. Soldiers and Ghosts: A History of Battle in Classical Greece. Random House, 2006.

Historical analysis of how Greek culture shaped Greek communication and conflict styles. Relevant to understanding Mediterranean approaches to argument.

Steele, Jonathan. Moscow Rules: Text and Subtext in Soviet Politics. Oxford University Press, 1994.

Explores how Soviet communication culture shaped Russian and Eastern European approaches to language, with emphasis on saying different things to different audiences. Informs analysis of Eastern European irony.

Mukerji, Chandra. Territorial Ambitions and the Gardens of Versailles. Cambridge University Press, 1997.

Cultural analysis of how spatial arrangements shape power and communication. Relevant to understanding how physical spaces (parliaments, dinner tables, boardrooms) shape conversation.

Bellah, Robert N., et al. Habits of the Heart: Individualism and Commitment in American Life. University of California Press, 1985.

Classic analysis of American culture and individualism. Essential background for understanding why American communication style privileges individual expression.

Bourdieu, Pierre. Distinction: A Social Critique of the Judgement of Taste. Harvard University Press, 1984.

Examines how taste, language use, and cultural capital function as markers of class. Relevant to understanding how speaking style signals social position.

Sennett, Richard. Respect in a World of Inequality. W.W. Norton, 2003.

Explores how respect functions in unequal societies and how communication patterns reflect and reinforce inequality. Informs discussion of power dynamics in conversation.

SPECIFIC STUDIES AND RESEARCH REFERENCED

Hastorf, Albert H. and Hadley Cantril. "They Saw a Game: A Case Study." Journal of Abnormal and Social Psychology, Vol. 49, 1954, pp. 129-134.

Classic study demonstrating that people from opposing groups perceive identical events differently based on tribal affiliation. Directly referenced in Chapter 1.

Moscovici, Serge. "Social Influence and Social Change." Academic Press, 1976.

Research on minority influence showing that consistent minority viewpoints can shift group consensus. Relevant to understanding how tribal opinion is formed and can be changed.

Baumeister, Roy F. and Mark R. Leary. "The Need to Belong: Desire for Interpersonal Attachments as a Fundamental Human Motivation." Psychological Bulletin, Vol. 117, No. 3, 1995, pp. 497-529.

Foundational research showing belonging is a fundamental human need. Explains why tribal exclusion is neurologically experienced as pain.

Putnam, Robert D. Bowling Alone: The Collapse and Revival of American Community. Simon & Schuster, 2000.

Demographic data on declining participation in community groups across America. Provides statistical foundation for argument about declining social connection.

PHILOSOPHICAL TEXTS

Habermas, Jürgen. The Theory of Communicative Action. Beacon Press, 1987.

Habermas' concept of "communicative action" (communication aimed at mutual understanding) vs. "strategic action" (communication aimed at persuasion) provides framework for distinguishing genuine dialogue from performance.

Austin, J.L. How to Do Things with Words. Oxford University

Press, 1962.

Speech act theory explains that language does not merely describe reality; it performs actions (promises, threats, declarations). Relevant to understanding how tribal language performs group cohesion.

Wittgenstein, Ludwig. Philosophical Investigations. Blackwell, 1953.

Wittgenstein's concept of "language games" (bounded systems where meaning is determined by context and use) illuminates how tribal communication operates as a closed system where meaning is shared internally.

Gadamer, Hans-Georg. Truth and Method. Seabury Press, 1975.

Gadamer's concept of "fusion of horizons" (how understanding occurs when different perspectives merge) is the philosophical foundation for genuine dialogue as opposed to tribal communication.

MEMOIRS AND JOURNALISM ON CULTURE AND CONVERSATION

Fenton, James. The Strength of Poetry. Oxford University Press, 2001.

Essay collection on language, poetry, and meaning. Includes observations on how different cultures approach language differently.

Didion, Joan. Slouching Towards Bethlehem. Farrar, Straus and Giroux, 1968.

Collection of essays demonstrating the power of careful observation of cultural behaviour. Informs the book's approach to cultural critique through close attention to actual behaviour.

Theroux, Paul. The Great Railway Bazaar. Houghton Mifflin, 1975.

Travel writing that carefully observes different cultures' communication styles. Relevant to understanding how language and manners vary globally.

Said, Edward W. Orientalism. Pantheon Books, 1978.

While not specifically about communication, Said's analysis of how Western representations shape understanding of other cultures informs critical approach to discussing non-Western cultures.

CONTEMPORARY CRITICISM AND CULTURAL COMMENTARY

Turkle, Sherry. Reclaiming Conversation: The Power of Talk in a Digital Age. Penguin Press, 2015.

Recent work specifically on how digital technology has eroded conversational capacity. Directly relevant to book's central argument.

Lanier, Jaron. Ten Arguments for Deleting Your Social Media Accounts Right Now. Henry Holt, 2018.

Contemporary critique of social media from technologist perspective. Relevant to understanding structural reasons why social platforms encourage performance over presence.

Harris, Tristan. "Technology Is Hijacking Your Attention." filmed at TEDxBoulder, November 2014.

While not a book, Harris's TED talk on "attention economy" has been influential in framing how technology shapes communication. Relevant to understanding algorithmic incentives.

Twenge, Jean M. iGen: Why Today's Super-Connected Kids Are Growing Up Less Rebellious, More Tolerant, More Anxious—and Completely Unprepared for Adulthood. Atria Books, 2017.

Data on generational differences in communication and social patterns. Relevant to understanding how digital communication is shaping a generation's conversational capacity.

RESEARCH ON SPECIFIC CULTURAL PHENOMENA

Hendricks, Aart. "Silence as a Cultural and Communicative Phenomenon." Intercultural Communication Studies, Vol. 16, No. 1, 2007.

Research-based examination of how silence functions differently across cultures. Directly relevant to Chapter 10 analysis.

LeBaron, Michelle. Bridging Cultural Conflicts: A New Approach for a Changing World. Jossey-Bass, 2002.

Framework for understanding how cultural differences in communication style create conflict. Relevant to analysis of cross-cultural misunderstandings.

Ting-Toomey, Stella. Communicating Across Cultures. Guilford Press, 1999.

Examines how face-saving concerns drive communication differently across cultures. Directly relevant to analysis of Asian, Middle Eastern, and Mediterranean communication styles.

PSYCHOLOGY OF CONFIDENCE AND CERTAINTY

Dunning, David and Justin Kruger. "Unskilled and Unaware of It: How Difficulties in Recognizing One's Own Incompetence Lead to Inflated Self-Assessments." Journal of Personality and Social Psychology, Vol. 77, No. 6, 1999, pp. 1121-1134.

The "Dunning-Kruger Effect" research explaining why incompetent people are most confident. Directly relevant to Chapter 17 analysis of "The Cult of Confidence."

Gross, Daniel M. The Secret History of Emotion: From Aristotle's

Rhetoric to Modern Brain Science. University of Chicago Press, 2006.

Historical analysis of how understanding of emotion has changed. Relevant to understanding why confidence is neurologically linked to tribal belonging.

Festinger, Leon. A Theory of Cognitive Dissonance. Stanford University Press, 1957.

Classic theory explaining why people reject information that contradicts their beliefs. Foundational for understanding tribal resistance to outside information.

ACKNOWLEDGEMENTS

This book emerged from decades of observation across continents, countless conversations with brilliant minds, and the accumulated wisdom—and occasional foolishness—of people from dozens of cultures. It is impossible to acknowledge everyone who shaped these ideas, but I will attempt to thank those whose influence was most direct.

THE INSPIRATION

First, to Christoph, R., and M.—my conspirators at that particular lunch at Boodles, St. James's. Your exasperation with the endless "Back to Me" of modern conversation planted the seed from which this entire book grew. Your friendship, spanning decades, has been a laboratory for understanding how genuine dialogue works even when we disagree about nearly everything. Without that moment—that particular observation over that particular meal—this book would never have existed. This work is, in many ways, an extended meditation on why that lunch mattered: it was a genuine conversation between people who actually listened to each other.

INTELLECTUAL DEBT

I am indebted to the scholars and researchers whose work forms the intellectual backbone of this book. Erving Goffman taught me to see conversation as performance and performance as real. Deborah Tannen showed me that communication style is not universal. Edward Hall's work on high-context and low-context communication was foundational for understanding cultural differences. Haidt's work on moral tribalism and Sunstein's analysis of group polarisation shaped my understanding of why tribal thinking is so powerful. Türkle and Pariser's work on digital technology informed my analysis of how platforms reshape conversation.

Particularly, I am grateful to the researchers whose work on listening, silence, and reflection provided counterweight to the noise. Michael Nichols' work on listening was essential, as was Walter Ong's historical analysis of how technology changes thought. These voices reminded me that the solution to our communication crisis is not more technology but a return to older skills.

PEOPLE AND PLACES

I am grateful to the many people across the world who taught me how their cultures approach conversation, argument, listening, and silence.

In Moscow, Warsaw, and Prague—colleagues who modelled how Eastern European realism infuses communication.

In Stockholm and Copenhagen—mentors who showed me that restraint and silence can be forms of power.

In London—the British friends and colleagues who demonstrated how irony and understatement can contain more truth than direct statement.

In Paris—thinkers who showed me that conversation can be philosophy, that style and substance are not opposites.

In Rome and Barcelona—warmth that reminded me that passion in argument need not mean disconnection from the other person.

In Cairo and Damascus—hosts who taught me that hospitality and dignity shape communication as much as content.

In Lagos and Johannesburg—storytellers who showed me that rhythm and collective memory shape how people listen.

In Tokyo and Delhi—teachers who demonstrated that restraint and multiplicity can coexist.

In New York and Los Angeles—the relentless optimists whose confidence, annoying as it is sometimes, contains genuine faith in human possibility.

PROFESSIONAL COLLABORATORS

I am grateful to The Writers Collective for believing in this project when it was merely an observation at lunch. To my editors, who pushed me to clarify and deepen. To colleagues at DVC Consultants who lived with my observations about communication culture for years. To the teams I have worked with across continents who, through our disagreements and attempts at understanding across cultural lines, taught me most of what I know about how real dialogue works.

PERSONAL THANKS

To my ex-wives and girlfriends, who taught me more about listening, or the failure of it, than any book could. To my son, who demonstrated that genuine listening is possible and that it requires humility. To my friends across continents who maintain conversation across time zones and difference through genuine curiosity about how the other person sees the world. To my parents, who modelled different approaches to communication—my mother's warmth and immediate engagement, my father's (eventual) thoughtfulness and carefully chosen words.To my step-mother for her patience and encouragement. To my grandfather, Rear Admiral Robert Love Alexander, who taught me through family stories that leadership sometimes means knowing when to listen rather than command.He was one of lifes very wise and considered people.

QUENTIN DRUMMOND ANDERSON

THE UNACKNOWLEDGED

There are countless people—taxi drivers in Istanbul, baristas in Berlin, exotic dancers in Moscow, colleagues in conference rooms, strangers on trains—whose observations about how people fail to listen became part of this book's fabric. To them, I offer thanks that they will never read. Their lives and words shaped these observations about how we all talk without listening.

AND FINALLY

To the reader: You are reading this book, which means you are already participating in the solution. The very act of reading a book about listening is an act of listening—to my voice, to ideas different from your own, to the possibility that you might be wrong about how well you listen. By staying with this argument through 20 chapters, you have already demonstrated the capacity for the very thing this book argues we have lost: the willingness to engage with someone else's full thought, even when you disagree.

The hope of this book is not that you will remember every argument I have made. The hope is that you will close it, and the next time you are in conversation with someone who thinks differently than you do, you will pause. You will listen. You will resist the urge to interrupt. You will ask a genuine question and wait for a real answer.

That moment—that pause, that genuine listening—is the revolution this book is asking for.

Thank you for taking the time to listen.

NOTE ON RESEARCH METHODOLOGY

This book draws on five decades of personal observation across continents, combined with synthesis of published research in psychology, neuroscience, anthropology, cultural studies, and communication. The cultural observations are drawn from lived experience—years spent in different countries, professional work across cultural contexts, and close relationships with people from diverse backgrounds.

The scientific claims about neurobiology, psychology, and sociology are drawn from the academic literature cited in these sources. Where specific studies are referenced in the text, they are noted above. The book does not make scientific claims it cannot defend, but it acknowledges that space limitations required condensing complex research into brief references. Readers interested in deeper engagement with specific claims are encouraged to consult the original research.

The cultural analysis is necessarily generalised. Within every culture mentioned there is enormous variation—regional, generational, class-based, individual. The observations are about general patterns, tendencies, and common characteristics —not universal truths. A Brazilian may not resemble the Brazilian described here; a Swede may be far more expressive than the stereotype suggests. But patterns exist, and they shape how communities of people approach communication generally.

The personal anecdotes and examples are drawn from observation of real interactions, but have been adjusted to protect privacy and are often composite examples rather than direct transcriptions of actual conversations. The spirit of the interactions is preserved; the specific details are sometimes altered.

The book's arguments about technology and social media are current as of late 2025. The digital landscape changes rapidly, and some specific references to platform mechanics, algorithm features, or corporate structures may become outdated. The underlying arguments about attention economy, algorithmic amplification of outrage, and the structural incentives against genuine listening should remain relevant longer.

Finally, this book is not claiming to be the complete, objective truth about how people communicate globally. It is one person's informed perspective, shaped by particular experiences and particular intellectual traditions. The reader will undoubtedly find examples that do not match their experience. I invite those disagreements and contradictions. They are opportunities for genuine dialogue—the very thing this book argues for.

Printed in Great Britain
by Amazon

05c29469-0112-449c-b8c0-f83525902df8R01